Compiled by Everett Ofori

SUCCESS TIPS FROM SUCCESSFUL AFRICAN AMERICANS

Volume 1

SUCCESS TIPS FROM SUCCESSFUL AFRICAN AMERICANS

VOLUME 1

Everett Ofori

© Everett Ofori, 2022

All rights reserved. No part of this publication may be reproduced, stored in a retrieval system, or transmitted, in any form or by any means, without the prior permission in writing of Everett Ofori (everettoforijapan@gmail.com), or as expressly permitted by law, or under terms agreed with the appropriate reprographics rights organization.

ISBN: 1-894221-14-1   ISBN 13: 978-1-894221-14-6

OTHER BOOKS BY EVERETT OFORI

1. Succeeding From the Margins of Canadian Society: A Strategic Resource for New Immigrants, Refugees and International Students. Written by Dr. Francis Adu-Febiri and Everett Ofori, 2009 – ISBN 978-1-926585-27-7
2. Read Assure: Guaranteed Formula for Reading Success with Phonics, 2010 – ISBN 978-1894221054
3. Guaranteed Formula for Public Speaking Success, 2011 – ISBN 978-1894221078
4. 3,570 Real-world English Phrases for Speaking & Writing Practice (Vol. 1), 2011 – ISBN 978-1894221125
5. 3,570 Real-world English Phrases for Speaking & Writing Practice (Vol. 2), 2011 – ISBN 978-1894221139
6. Prepare for Greatness: How to Make Your Success Inevitable, 2013 – ISBN 13: 978-0921143000
7. The Changing Japanese Woman: From *Yamatonadeshiko* to *YamatonadeGucci*, 2013 – ISBN 13: 978-1894221047
8. The Global Student's Companion: 10,001 Timeless Themes & Topics for Dialogue, Discussion & Debate Practice. Compiled by Everett Ofori, 2015 – ISBN 13: 978-1-894221-02-3
9. Guaranteed Formula for Effective Business Writing, 2017 – ISBN 978-1894221108
10. English Language Mastermind: From Confident Communication to Higher Test Scores, 2018 – ISBN 978-1894221160
11. Guaranteed Formula for Writing Success, 2019 – ISBN 978-1-926918-22-8
12. Guaranteed Formula for Writing Effective Business Emails & Letters, 2019 – ISBN 978-1894221061
13. Guaranteed Formula for Effective Meeting Facilitation and Participation, 2020 – ISBN 978-1894221085

Introduction

Many thanks to all the professionals who responded with great cheerfulness to my call to share the secrets of their success.

Some might have had to interrupt other important personal and professional demands in order to give their full attention to this task.

The generous hearts with which they either spoke to me or wrote these nuggets shine through this volume. I hope that those of us who are the beneficiaries of such wisdom and insights will accept them, not blindly, but with attention, turn them over in our minds, and take action towards our own most cherished goals.

In some cases, it was not lost on me that this project connected with some threads of African-American history. For example, I believe that the lessons that Honorable Mary K. Bush shares from an era where some of her friends lost their lives to the bombs of racists, can fortify a new generation of Black children and others as they navigate their own novel pathways to success.

Also, as the importance of science and technology has come to dominate thinking in this early part of the 21st century, it is gratifying that the voices of inventors and entrepreneurs, medical doctors and researchers feature in the following pages.

Final thanks to Mr. Emory Georges, Mr. Kris Esplin, and Mr. Charles Acquah for advice on a multitude of miscellaneous matters; Ms. Ineko Hatake, my Japanese language instructor; and Dr. James Edward Fischer, Mr. Garry Krimotat, and Mr. John Cunningham for periodic words of encouragement.

To all readers, let's learn, think, and take action!

- Everett Ofori
 July 2022
 Tokyo, Japan

It Takes A Village - Let's Support these Worthy Causes suggested by Contributors to this book

1. **A Long Walk Home**
   1658 N. Milwaukee Ave.
   Suite 104
   Chicago, IL
   60647 USA
   https://www.alongwalkhome.org/
   info@alongwalkhome.org
   *Empowering young people to end violence against girls and women

2. **Capital Partners for Education**
   https://www.cpfe.org/our-organization/
   *Mentoring low-income high school and college students in the academic middle from the Washington, D.C. area to provide the skills and experiences they need to complete college successfully and to excel in the workforce

3. **Caring About People With Enthusiasm (CAPE) Legacy Fund, Inc.**
   www.claracares.com
   *Brigadier General Clara Adams-Ender, Executive Director

4. **Creative Arts, Inc.**
   9409 Kempton Ave.
   Cleveland, OH
   44108-2940 USA
   *Dr. Harrison Leslie Adams

5. **Dawn D. Bennett-Alexander Inclusive Community Award**
   University of Georgia (UGA)
   https://diversity.uga.edu/opportunities/awards/dawn_ba_inclusive_community_award
   *Honors faculty who promote diversity, equity, and inclusion

6. **Development Office at the Lincoln University of Pennsylvania for the Ivory V. Nelson Endowed Scholarship in Chemistry**
   Kymberly Truman Graves, J.D.
   Director of Major & Planned Gifts
   1570 Baltimore Pike
   Lincoln University, PA
   19352 USA
   *Kgraves@lincoln.edu (Email)

7. **Good Foundations Tutoring Service**
   3516 A Manor Drive, Vicksburg, MS, 39180 USA
   *Scholarship fund - provides assistance to families in need of funds to pay for weekly tutoring

8. **House of Umoja**
   5625 Master St.
   Philadelphia, PA
   19131 USA
   *A family-centered organization that acts as a primary human support for youth

9. **Ile Ase Ire**
   PO Box 315
   Walkertown, North Carolina
   USA 27051 USA
   http://www.Aselre.com/
   contact@aseire.com
   *Learn, grow, and connect

10. **Kingmakers of Oakland**
    www.kingmakersofoakland.org
    *Unapologetically focusing on Black boys (Engage, Encourage, Empower)

11. **Museum of African American Technology (MAAT)**
    Science Village,
    722 Chester Street, Oakland, CA
    94607 USA

12. **New Orleans Women and Children's Shelter (NOWCS)**
    2020 Liberty St.
    New Orleans, LA 70113 USA
    *Assisting homeless families in their darkest times

13. **New York School of Interior Design**
    https://www.nysid.edu/ways-to-give
    *Experts at preparing interior designers for professional success

14. **People's Programs**
    http://www.peoplesprograms.com
    *People's Breakfast Oakland;
     People's Community Health;
     Legal Support & Bail Program

15. **The Beck Cultural Exchange Center**
    1927 Dandridge Avenue
    Knoxville, Tennessee, 37915 USA
    www.beckcenter.net
    *The Mission of Beck is to be the place where Black history and culture are preserved, taught, and continued.

16. **The Black Association at Salk (BAS)**
    https://www.salk.edu/about/equity-inclusion/affinity-groups/
    *Maintaining a space of unity for the existing Black members of Salk Institute

17. **The Black Experience**
    Leadership/History
    https://www.theblackexperience.us/
    *Creating free positive educational content for all and connecting global audiences with stories of success

18. **The Center for Creativity and Inquiry**
    c/o Innovations International
    www.creativityandinquiry.org/

19. **The Daryl Cumber Dance Educational Travel Fund**
    Office of Institutional Advancement,
    Virginia State University, Virginia State University, VA 23806, USA
    (804) 524-5559

20. **The Jackie Joyner Kersee Boys & Girls Club**
    East St. Louis, Illinois
    https://www.bgca.org/about-us/alumni-hall-of-fame/jackie-joyner
    *Supports a club facility where young people can nurture their athletic talents

21. **The PETNA Foundation**
    2605 Camino Tassajara #2181
    Danville, CA 94526 USA
    https://www.petna.org/
    *Provides hands-on support to students and families in communities around the world

22. **The Privilege Institute**
    1794 Allouez Avenue, Suite C260,
    Green Bay, WI 54311 USA
    www.theprivilegeinstitute.com
    *Provides challenging collaborative and comprehensive strategies to empower and equip people to work for equity and justice

23. **The Reginald F. Lewis Museum**
    830 E. Pratt Street,
    Baltimore, MD
    21202 USA
    Tel: (443) 263-1814

24. **Us Against Alzheimer's**
    https://www.usagainstalzheimers.org/networks/african-americans#
    *Finding effective treatments and the prevention steps to stop Alzheimer's

Dedicated to my nephew, James Reynolds, who taught me a few things

"If you can think well, plan well, write well, and speak well, you have all that you need to change the course of human history - or at least - your own history."
- Everett Ofori

CONTENTS

CHAPTER 1	14	**DARYL CUMBER DANCE** TELLING OUR STORY
CHAPTER 2	20	**NIC BRATHWAITE** COMPETENCE & CHARACTER
CHAPTER 3	35	**TAMLA TURNER** FOLLOWING MY HEART
CHAPTER 4	39	**K. DAVID BOYER** PRIDE: THE DOUBLE-EDGED SWORD
CHAPTER 5	47	**TERRI FREEMAN** INSTITUTIONS LAST SIGNIFICANTLY LONGER
CHAPTER 6	51	**EDDIE MOORE, JR.** CHANGE IS POSSIBLE
CHAPTER 7	55	**DAWN D. BENNETT-ALEXANDER** PRACTICAL DIVERSITY

CHAPTER 8	60	**VADA O'HARA MANAGER** THE THREE 'C' PRINCIPLES
CHAPTER 9	68	**CORNELIA SHIPLEY** BE CLEAR ABOUT 'WHAT' AND 'HOW'
CHAPTER 10	72	**GARY S. MAY** THE POWER OF PERSISTENCE
CHAPTER 11	76	**PAULETTE R. IRONS** YOU CAN DO IT
CHAPTER 12	80	**KEVIN WAYNE JOHNSON** A CHANGED LIFE
CHAPTER 13	87	**ALICIA MCGEACHY** TAKE STOCK OF MYSELF
CHAPTER 14	92	**DELANO LEWIS** KNOW YOUR 'END GAME'
CHAPTER 15	97	**ESTELLA NEIZER-ASHUN** MY 5 A.M. PRAYER.
CHAPTER 16	102	**OGBONNA HAGINS** MAXIMIIZE LIFE
CHAPTER 17	109	**FALAKA FATTAH** GOD'S EYE PERSPECTIVE

CHAPTER 18	114	**H. LESLIE ADAMS** FOCUS ON BROADER GOALS
CHAPTER 19	118	**ELLEN GRANT** SERVANT LEADERSHIP
CHAPTER 20	122	**REJJI P. HAYES** COMPETENCE, WORK ETHIC, & INTEGRITY
CHAPTER 21	135	**LAURA HODGES** EACH NEW DAY, A NEW OPPORTUNITY
CHAPTER 22	139	**ANTHONY K. WUTOH** UNIVERSAL TRUTHS I LEARNED AS A CHILD
CHAPTER 23	143	**LINDSEY CAMERON** FIERCELY DEDICATED TO MY PATH
CHAPTER 24	147	**SAMUEL BUXTON** JOY AND PLEASURE IN SMALL AND REGULAR WINS
CHAPTER 25	152	**FRANCES WHITE HALL** NO SHORTCUTS TO SUCCESS
CHAPTER 26	156	**ALDRIN GOMES** MY GREATEST STRENGTH IS MY OPTIMISM
CHAPTER 27	161	**AUSTIN COLEY** THE KOBE BRYANT MENTALITY: "THE BEST SHOT, IS THE NEXT SHOT."

CHAPTER 28	165	**CLARA L. ADAMS-ENDER** SKILLS: READING, SPEAKING, AND WRITING
CHAPTER 29	169	**SOLOMON MENSAH** BEING THE BEST: MAKING IT IMPOSSIBLE TO BE IGNORED
CHAPTER 30	182	**DARIUS B. DAWSON** FOCUS ON SOCIAL RESPONSIBILITIES AND SERVICES
CHAPTER 31	187	**KIRK MCDONALD** DON'T USE SOMEONE ELSE'S RULER TO MEASURE YOUR SUCCESS
CHAPTER 32	192	**CHRISTOPHER BOONE** AN INSATIABLE HUNGER FOR KNOWLEDGE & INFORMATION
CHAPTER 33	210	**JOSEPH A. BAILEY II** "ME/WE"
CHAPTER 34	268	**BILL GUILLORY** 100% PERSONAL RESPONSIBILITY
CHAPTER 35	273	**KRISTEN L. POPE** THE WORLD, NEEDS YOU!
CHAPTER 36	280	**JEREMY CUTTS** I'M BUILT FOR STRUGGLE
CHAPTER 37	286	**WILLIAM A. LESTER, JR.** HOLD FAST TO DREAMS

CHAPTER 38	290	**GEORGE HOFSTETTER** TRUST, CULTIVATION, & INNER CURIOSITY
CHAPTER 39	296	**IVORY V. NELSON** EDUCATION MUST GLORY IN THE PRIVILEGE OF DOUBT
CHAPTER 40	313	**MARY K. BUSH** GIVING IT MY ALL
	324	**INDEX**
	328	**ABOUT THE EDITOR**

Daryl Cumber Dance

Telling Our Story

CHAPTER ONE

Dr. Daryl Cumber Dance

Professor Emerita, University of Richmond & Virginia Commonwealth University, Richmond, Virginia

Daryl Cumber Dance is a literary scholar, genealogist, folklorist, and novelist. She earned a doctorate in English from the University of Virginia and has taught at various universities including an appointment in 2013 as the Sterling A. Brown Professor of English at Howard University.

The Warmth of the Human Voice

The Griot Mamadou declares in the African epic *Sundiata*, "Other peoples use writing to record the past, but this invention has killed the faculty of memory among them. They do not feel the past anymore, for writing lacks the warmth of the human voice."

My whole career has been dedicated to preserving the voices (the words, the proverbs, the stories, the tales,

> "I MAKE IT CLEAR THAT I NEED TO HEAR WHAT THEY HAVE TO SAY THROUGH WHAT I CALL 'RESPECTFUL LISTENING.'"

the songs, even the scores of remarkable exclamations [chuckles, whoops, moans, hollers] of special folk in African Diaspora communities. I have compiled collections of African American and Caribbean folklore; of African American women's humor; of family history; of the memorates of prisoners involved in one of the most amazing prison escapes in American history; and of interviews with writers and with people who knew those writers. I have represented a range of voices of African American characters in two novels and a collection of short stories.

I have had notable success in my endeavors. Everyone is amazed at the authenticity of the voices. Everyone repeatedly asks how I get people to open up and share their stories with me. The answer is simple.

I listen.

Indeed, the greatest skill that I have developed that has brought me whatever success I have enjoyed in my career as a teacher, folklorist, literary scholar, genealogist, novelist, and student of African Diaspora culture is listening. The critical substance of the thirteen books and scores of essays that I have written was obtained through interviews and conversations. Though a great deal of reading and research was required to prepare myself to conduct the requisite interviews, the basic material that would represent my unique contributions came mainly from the information that I would gather from my sources.

The greatest key to success in this kind of field work is winning the confidence of the informant. First of all, I approach my subjects with a proper humility and with respect. I make it clear that I need to hear what they have to say through what I call "respectful listening," a kind of listening that communicates an appreciation of the informants' intelligence, their mother wit, their situation, their culture, their values, their artistry, their eloquence. Though I come with prepared questions, I do not interrupt my informants if they vary the conversation. Perhaps we spend some time on what I might have originally deemed irrelevant chatter, but I often come away with some gem that I didn't even know to ask about.

Finally, what I found when I listened, truly listened, to the folk sayings, the folk tales, the folk songs, the folk idioms, was that I heard some forgotten echoes of myself and my own past. I felt the reality of the power of atavism. There was a sense of self-discovery, of exaltation, of kinship such as one experiences when viewing a painting or reading a book that touches that inexplicable something that connects. This is communication and this is one of the important rewards of creative, respectful listening. This is the fulfillment of the *Ifa* divination, "Speak to me so that I may speak to you. By our voices we recognize each other in the darkness." And so through the years I have listened and recorded, listened and learned, listened and reveled in the warmth of human voices. Then, with pen in hand, I try with scholarly rigor, intellectual honesty, cultural integrity, and whatever artistry and eloquence I possess to create my own narrative as truthfully and as responsibly and as powerfully as I can. This is perhaps the most difficult part. I labor under the burden of the heavy sense of responsibility I feel to those whom I have recorded, to those whose voices I still hear in my head, to those about whom I am writing, to the many griots who have shared their narratives with me.

Each of my works ultimately becomes "our story."

Here is a list of Professor Dance's publications:

- *Shuckin' and Jivin': Folklore from Contemporary Black Americans, 1978*
- *Folklore from Contemporary Jamaicans, 1985*
- *Fifty Caribbean Writers: A Bio-Bibliographical and Critical Sourcebook, 1986*
- *Long Gone: The Mecklenburg Six and the Theme of Escape in Black Folklore, 1987*
- *New World Adams: Conversations with Contemporary West Indian Writers, 1992*
- *Honey, Hush! An Anthology of African American Women's Humor, 1998*
- *The Lineage of Abraham: The Biography of a Free Black Family in Charles City, VA, 1998*
- *From My People: 400 Years of African American Folklore, 2002*
- *In Search of Annie Drew, the Mother and Muse of Jamaica Kincaid, 2016*
- *Till Death Us Did Part: A Story of Four Widows, 2020*
- *Land of the Free....Negroes: A Historical Novel, 2020*
- *Here Am I: Miscellaneous Meanderings, Meditations, Memoirs, and Melodramas, 2020*

Notes & Reflections

> " I'VE LEARNED THAT PEOPLE WILL FORGET WHAT YOU SAID, PEOPLE WILL FORGET WHAT YOU DID, BUT PEOPLE WILL NEVER FORGET HOW YOU MADE THEM FEEL. "
>
> **- DR. MAYA ANGELOU**

2

Nic Brathwaite

Competence and Character

CHAPTER TWO

Dr. Nicholas Brathwaite

Engineer, Investor, Philanthropist, Celesta Capital, San Francisco, CA

Dr. Brathwaite, founder and managing partner at Celesta Capital, has patented a number of inventions, some of which are used in low-cost cell phones. He has built several businesses that have grown revenues into the millions and billions of dollars. He serves on the Board of Directors of companies around the world, from his home base in the United States, through Argentina, Brazil, and India, to Japan, where he is Chairman of the Board of a Japanese organization.

Prepare for Success

I'll be honest with you. I can't say my desire to be successful was something that I always had. Even when I went to university, I did it just to get a degree. I've always felt that getting a degree was something you do. If you're in school long enough, you should be able to get a degree. So for me, I went to university with the intention of being prepared for success. The idea of being successful, the idea of being good, the idea of being among the best in the world at what you did, was always a driver for me. In fact, it was such a driver for me that when I look back, I never celebrated graduating from high school; in our family, that was expected. There was no celebration for graduating from high school.

In fact, I didn't even go to my undergraduate graduation ceremony, to walk across the stage to get my degree. I didn't participate in that because I had already moved on to graduate school. I started graduate school less than a week after I finished my final exams; I had already moved on because to me that was a stepping stone. I did not need to celebrate. I was on my way to bigger things. So, I believe that the desire to be successful and to be good at what I was doing was always there, but I didn't know what that looked like. I didn't have any preconceived idea of what that success would look like.

> "I BELIEVE THAT SUCCESS SHOULD BE MEASURED PRIMARILY ON THE IMPACT ONE HAS ON OTHER PEOPLE, OR ON YOUR COMMUNITY, MORE THAN ON ANYTHING ELSE."

Education: Consider Your Options

If you look at the rate at which the cost of education has increased, it seems to have increased at a much faster rate than people's salaries have increased. So, for many people, the cost of education has become extremely high and for many careers, they don't make enough money after they graduate to be able to pay back that debt that they would've built. People have to consider not just the cost of the education, but their opportunities, that is, the income opportunities after they graduate. If you're going to be very successful in the high-tech industry, it's going to be very difficult for you to do that without going through the kind of studies that are traditionally offered. I think people have to look at things differently. One can argue that instead of going to the most expensive undergraduate school, maybe, you go to the best high school; you get a good foundation there and then go to a state university, which is much less expensive, where you don't have to rack up huge debts in order to get your first undergraduate degree. And then, you look to get a scholarship to graduate school, and that's where you can choose one of the more prestigious schools, and thus, control the cost that way. And by the way, if you go to some of these less expensive schools, there's a good chance that your performance might be better, and that might help you to get a scholarship to a high-end graduate school. And your overall costs will be lower, or you can go to a community college before you go to university and then transfer. So, I think, there are alternatives to just saying, let me just do a two-year diploma, or let me just take some classes. But for some professions, that might be the right approach. In the end, one has to look at it profession by profession to decide what might be most appropriate.

Don't Focus on the Hurdles
There are always barriers to anything and it's not always easy to determine what the source of the barriers are. I look at it more like hurdles. I have a friend who ran hurdles at a very high level. And he explained to me one time, when I was in high school, and I tried to run the hurdles, and I couldn't even get over the first one. My friend told me that the key to getting over these hurdles is to keep your eyes focused on the finish line, and then just having a rhythm that navigates these hurdles as you come to them. But if you focus on the hurdles, then it's very difficult. And so, that was the problem I was having. I was running and looking at the hurdles and figuring out how to get over them. And that scared me. I have taken the same approach in my career, which

is to not focus on the hurdles, but to focus on the objective and then navigate the hurdles as you get to them. So just as you might watch a 400-meter hurdler run and look effortless as they take their three or four strides, and then just hop over and take their three or four strides, and hop over, it might appear to be like that: the hurdles are there and you have to navigate them as you come to them.

Don't Stand on the Sidelines

I was once asked in an interview I did for *Profile* magazine how I navigate challenges such as racial prejudice. One of the things I said to them was, it's hard for me to determine when you come across some of these hurdles, whether it's racially based or not. I don't spend a lot of time trying to figure that out because when you run into these challenges, it's hard to tell. It's hard to tell if something is racially based or if it's because they don't like you for other things: being from the Caribbean, maybe they don't like my accent. Maybe they don't like my size. There are a lot of different things people may not like, and sometimes we're quick to judge, to jump on and play the race card. I am hesitant to do that, even though there are a couple of cases, not so much in my career, but in my life experience where I've experienced racism that I know for sure was racism. In a business context, it's not always easy to determine that something is a matter of racism. I do believe that I have been put in many situations where in order for me to be successful, I had to perform much better than the competition. I could just be slightly better than the competition, for whatever the reason.

The approach that I've always taken is that you can't win the game if you stand on the outside, on the sidelines, and complain about the rules. There is no benefit to just standing on the sidelines and complaining about how unfair the rules are. The only way to win is to get in the game.

I have taken the position that you just tell me what the rules are, and I'll figure out what I have to do; I will do what I need to do in order to win. If that means I have to be twice as good as the next person, then I'm going to go try to be twice as good as the next person. Instead of sitting around and complaining, I'm going to get in the game and go try to win it. That's the approach that I've taken.

No matter what the hurdles are, no matter what the issues may be, I am not just going to sit on the sideline and complain. I'm going to go try to compete, figure out what I need to do and go do what I need to do to compete and win.

I played a little bit of sports in high school and college. In sports, one team always has a competitive advantage. One team might have home court advantage or home field advantage, or they might have one superstar who is better than everybody on your team. You have to go and overcome those disadvantages, those competitive advantages that they may have.

Similarly, in my career, I understand that I might have some disadvantages and I have to overcome them by being really good, that is, by making sure I own the advantages that I have so I could perform above and beyond and overcome whatever disadvantages that may exist.

Team Building: Consider Competence and Character

I believe that in building teams, competence is extremely important. Some people focus primarily on loyalty, or they focus on how much they like the person. That is important too, but I prioritize competence. And then I work on the other elements as well. If you can find somebody who's competent, loyal and has other great attributes, that's the best. But I focus first on competence, and I also believe that character is important. So, in building a team, you want to have competent people with good character. You want to have people who trust and believe in you and what you're trying to do and people that you can trust.

Now, that doesn't mean that the trust is always there. You can't start with the trust. Sometimes you have to build the trust. In many of the things I've done, I have gone back and brought people on to start with me that I've done stuff with before: we know each other, we understand each other and they believe in me and what I'm trying to do, and they share the same objectives.

As you move up, it's really important for you to try to attract people who really believe in the objective. The highest compliment a leader can get is when people want to be associated with that leader, not because of what the leader has done or what the leader can do for them, but because of who the leader is. I have tried to live my life and work with people who believe in me, people who value my character and value being associated with me and the things I'm trying to do. With that, number one, you get people who are committed to both the objective and to supporting you. And they could be honest with you. They could be brutally honest with you. I see among many people, especially minorities, Black people, sometimes you're afraid to surround yourself with super bright people. And I'm not afraid of that.

I have enough confidence in my own ability that I don't mind surrounding myself with people who may know more than me in certain areas. In fact, that's what I want. I want people who are brighter than me in some areas. I have enough confidence in my abilities that I don't have to feel like I am the brightest person in the room on every single topic. And so I want to surround myself with people who are smarter than me in many areas. And oftentimes, what I bring more than anything else, especially in the technology world, is breadth. I bring breadth and vision. And then I hire people who have the depth in certain areas that I may lack. And of course, they're going to be smarter than me in those areas. I'm the one who can tie all of the pieces together laterally, while I go get people who are deeper than me vertically. And so I think by getting breadth, as well as the depth, you create great teams.

Face Issues Head-on
When I see something that I know is likely to be a problem, I'm not afraid to address it. Oftentimes, the challenge people have is that you see red flags or you see issues, but if the person, for example, is very good at what they do, you tend to ignore some of the character issues. So, as I said, competence is important. But it's not so important that I would say character doesn't matter. I think the two together are important. So, even if a person is supremely competent but also has lousy character, I would say it's probably not the right person. And I'm not afraid to make those decisions and take the chance of finding somebody that may be slightly less competent, but with much better character.

We all have strengths and weaknesses. It's usually a combination of things that is a problem rather than one or two. So, I don't like to have a single litmus test. I look at the character, at the combination of their trustworthiness and honesty and other elements that are important, because you have to be able to trust the person. But I think a lot of those things are also tied in with the person's belief in the objectives and the person's trust and confidence in you as well. That's why it's hard to just do a litmus test because there are things that interact.

You're Always Working for Somebody

I'm in the investment business. We started our own firm; we have a partnership. Four of us are partners in this, so we are co-owners. I don't really look at it from an owner-employee perspective. I actually don't look at things that way, because even when I worked in big public companies, like Intel, or when you start a company, you have people you're responsible to. So for example, as an investment firm, most of the money in the firm comes from other people. And so, in a way you work for those people. I mean, to me, you're always working for somebody.

I tell young entrepreneurs when they come to me, especially African Americans, or Black people in general. Sometimes, I would ask them, "Why do you want to start your own business?" And oftentimes, they will say things like, "Well, I want to work for myself. I don't want to work for anybody." And I would say, "Well then, I can't invest in your business. Because if I invest in your business, you have to work for me too." So I don't look at it that way. I believe that in everything you do, there are stakeholders that you are to go to. Even in my own life, I look at things that way, that as a Christian, God is looking over what I'm doing. And I'm hoping that I do things in a way that would please him.

So, whether you're an investor where you're investing other people's money, you have to be thinking of working for those people that have invested in you, because your job is to make good returns for them. And when you run a business, when you run a public company, you have the investors in the company, who are stakeholders in you; you have an obligation to perform in a way that will bring value to your stakeholders.

Obviously, as you move up in an organization, you have greater levels of responsibility, but you have greater levels of accountability as well. I don't look at a business in terms of working for somebody versus working for yourself, in the typical way people look at that.

The Child's Real Potential
As a child, I never realized I had a bent for technology until I got there and I looked back. And then I could see how it all made sense. When I was growing up in the Caribbean, I was a very good student. And back in those days, we didn't have a lot of employment opportunities. I suspect it would be the same in places like Ghana, where, if you were bright, everybody told you that you had to be a lawyer, a doctor, or something of the sort. But the number of professions you had were not that great.

When I was growing up, the professionals I knew were lawyers, doctors, teachers, nurses, accountants, and others like that. I didn't know very many engineers. I had an uncle who was an engineer. I didn't really know what he did. So, growing up, I never had a desire to be an engineer. But growing up, everybody would tell me I should be a doctor. And so that's what I absorbed. So even when I went to university, my goal initially was to study medicine. But after my first year at university, I realized I didn't like biology, and it's hard to be a doctor if you don't like biology. But when I look back, I realize physics was my favorite subject. And I really wanted to study physics, but I didn't know any physicists. The only people I knew who had degrees in physics were people who taught me in high school and I knew I didn't want to be a teacher. So, I thought the only thing you could do with physics was to teach; I didn't know anybody who was a physicist who did anything. I decided: I like physics, I like chemistry and I like mathematics. With that, I decided I'm going to do something that combined those things.

Looking back, when I was about nine years old, my dad bought me a physics set. And at nine years old, I figured out how to create a doorbell. I think there was a chapter in a book, something that talked about making a doorbell. We had a small house; I wired a doorbell in my parents' house. I put a doorbell in at 9 years old. I had this kind of acumen, but I didn't fully realize the potential. I should have known that I wasn't supposed to be a doctor too, because I never liked hospitals. I never liked blood. I remember when I was about 16, one of my uncles, a doctor, took me to the hospital to do some rounds at the hospital with him. He took me into a room where they were going to be doing surgery. I went into the room and I started feeling sick, like I was going to faint. And so, they escorted me out of the room, and while they were escorting me out of the room, they were just bringing in the patient. I was feeling sick and faint even before the patient was in the room! So, clearly, I wasn't really cut out for that.

Even though I had decided not to pursue pre-med because of the biology stuff, at the end of my junior year, I did have an opportunity to consider medical school. I went to several of my professors at McMaster University, three of them actually, and asked them what they thought. All three of those professors told me that they thought I was a natural-born engineer or scientist and that they would recommend that's what I should do. They thought I should go to graduate school and continue with that and not do medicine. And it turns out that they were all scientists and technologists, so they might have been biased. But I took their advice. My dad also gave me some good advice. I asked my dad as well. And my dad said to me, "All your life, you were saying, you want to study medicine and now you're at this position where you're not sure; maybe, you should stick to what you're doing. Because if medicine was what you really wanted to do, you would be pursuing it and not be confused."

Definition of Success

I believe that success should be measured primarily on the impact one has on other people, or on your community, more than on anything else. This is because if you don't measure it that way, one could start confusing wealth or other things with success. I believe success should be measured based on impact, such as, impact on the lives of others. When I look at my own success, I look at what impact I have had on the lives of people and what impact I have had in the profession or the industry in which I work.

On the other hand, many people tend to look at success primarily based on what salary you make or how much money you make or where you live or what kind of car you drive. I don't necessarily believe that because you are wealthier than me, you're more successful. And I'll give you an example of that. I was in a discussion with some friends one time and these were guys who believed that money is everything and they were comparing two people and saying one person was more successful because they were worth billions of dollars. And the other person was not as successful because that person was worth hundreds of dollars. I told them that I completely disagreed because I saw it the other way. I said, as an example, if you have a person who started a company and it's some kind of social media, say, an internet company, and they grew the company to 20 people, and then sold it to Facebook or some other entity for 3 billion dollars. And that person ends up making 500 million dollars as an example. So, you have this company: it employed 20 people, and sold for 3 billion; this person was the leader. They made $500 million.

Now you have another company, and this company grew to be billions of dollars in revenue, employed 500,000 people and went public. The person who started the company made 50 million dollars. Which one is more successful? The one where the guy made 500 million dollars, but employed 20 people, or the one where the guy made 50 million dollars in the process and employed 500,000. To me, the latter is more successful because that person had a bigger impact on people's lives and on the community and on everything else. So, I believe that's the way success should be measured: based on the impact that you had on your industry, on the lives of other people, and the way you've helped other people.

Lifetime Learning

I went to school to learn how to learn. And so, for me, learning is a lifetime endeavor. I'm always learning. I'm always researching. I'm always trying to be better and more knowledgeable than I am today. And the more I learn, the more I realize how much I don't know, and the more it encourages me to want to know more. As I mentioned before, I'm motivated to make a difference. So, no matter what it is I'm working on, I want to make a difference. I also am motivated by the fact that, because I'm from a small island in the Caribbean or because I'm a Black person, I believe that I have the ability to impact how people think about people that look like me. I'm highly motivated to set a good example and to accomplish a lot in order to try to help influence the way people think of me and my race. In fact, I often talk about the fact that I am from a very small island. Although I'm from Grenada, I was born on a tiny island called Caille Island with a population of 7,000 people. Even though I never lived there, my parents were from there and I was born there. We moved when I was about three or four years old. But the reason I highlight that is because I remember

> "THE APPROACH THAT I'VE ALWAYS TAKEN IS YOU CAN'T WIN THE GAME IF YOU STAND ON THE OUTSIDE, ON THE SIDELINES, AND COMPLAIN ABOUT THE RULES."

when I was a kid growing up in Grenada, even though Grenada is not a big place itself, they used to talk down about people who came from that little island. I want to motivate people who come from those kinds of backgrounds, for them to realize that if I could be successful, they have a chance to be successful too. If you look at a lot of the things I do, I don't talk a lot about the schools I went to. Indeed, I went to two Canadian Ivy League schools (McMaster University and the University of Waterloo). But I don't talk a lot about that because it's easy for people to say that's why you're successful. And it's certainly a reason, it's part of it. But I talk about where I'm from, and the reason is that I want people to see me as just an ordinary person who was able to achieve certain things, which would motivate them to be able to achieve their own goals. If you talk mainly about the schools you went to, you might be sending a message that for you to be successful, you have to get these opportunities and not everybody gets those opportunities.

~~~

Dr. Brathwaite holds an honorary Doctor of Laws from McMaster University, Hamilton, Canada. Along with his wife, Janice, he has set up the PETNA Foundation, to support youth, education, and development endeavors.

Notes & Reflections

> "IT IS NOT ONLY THOSE WHO...DIE FOR THEIR COUNTRY WHO ARE HEROES. HEROES ARE BEING MADE EVERYDAY AND MOST OF THEM ARE NOT EVEN KNOWN. IF WE STRIVE FOR EXCELLENCE IN OUR AREA OF ENDEAVOR AND ARE WILLING TO MAKE SACRIFICES FOR THE BENEFIT OF OTHERS, EACH OF US CAN BECOME A HERO."
>
> **- AMELIA ADDAE**

3

Tamla Turner

Following My Heart

CHAPTER THREE

Tamla Turner, MS., CCC-SLP

Speech Language Pathologist, Turner Speech & Language Services

Tamla Turner provides in-home private therapy. In addition, she offers independent contract services, including assessment and treatment of articulation, speech sound disorders, language, swallowing, stuttering, voice, and cognitive impairments in all age categories. She earned a Bachelor of Science (B.S.) in Communicative Disorders from Arkansas State University and a Master of Science in Communicative Disorders (M.S.) from Jackson State University.

Following My Heart

I would like to begin by saying that I did not always understand the power that one possesses to change the pathway to growth. As a new graduate, I confused dedication and loyalty and found out how easy it can be to lose yourself in someone else's dream.

> "BELIEF IN WHAT I HAVE TO OFFER, DISCIPLINE, SELF-MOTIVATION, THE ABILITY TO NETWORK, COURAGE, AND MY FAITH HAVE CARRIED ME THUS FAR."

Around 2017, I was working for a large hospital providing services within an outpatient setting. I began to feel dissatisfied and unfulfilled in my professional growth. I began to feel as if I was supposed to be somewhere else, doing something else. I decided to take a leap of faith in the fall of 2018 and I started learning about contracts, insurance, billing, business structure, and marketing.

I began to feel this drive to move like never before. Finally, around the start of 2019, I launched my business and the rest is history. I can honestly say that I have learned so much about myself since deciding to follow my heart.

In my opinion, there are several traits that have helped me along the way. Belief in what I have to offer, discipline, self-motivation, the ability to network, courage, and my faith have carried me thus far. Knowing what I want, laying out a plan, and working hard to achieve my goals have been vital to helping my business. I've found that being flexible in how I respond to events that are out of my control is also important.

In my eyes, success is not just business growth. It is also personal growth. Every business wants to grow financially. However, it is important to remember that small steps lead to big gains too. Continuing your education is also key. My taking courses annually to learn about new modalities, recent technologies, and up-to-date research has been invaluable to being able to compete with others within my field. I plan to continue learning so that I can scale my business and continue to grow.

Notes & Reflections

> "WE ARE EACH OTHER'S HARVEST;
> WE ARE EACH OTHER'S BUSINESS;
> WE ARE EACH OTHER'S MAGNITUDE AND BOND."
>
> **- GWENDOLYN BROOKS**

4

K. David Boyer, Jr.

Pride:
The Double-Edged Sword

CHAPTER FOUR

K. David Boyer, Jr.

**Chairman & CEO,
GlobalWatch Technologies
Oakton, Virginia**

K. David Boyer leads strategic direction and oversees continued financial growth of a complex systems solutions provider that specializes in CyberSecurity, Business Intelligence, Information Management, and Systems Engineering.

Pride: The Double-edged Sword

Many thought leaders have shared their understanding of pride as a double-edged sword: simultaneously both a blessing and a sin.

For me, pride means self-respect, and I believe that it is the human need to think highly of oneself. As I reflect

> "WE ARE WHAT WE REPEATEDLY DO. EXCELLENCE, THEN, IS NOT AN ACT, BUT A HABIT AND A WAY OF LIFE."
>
> - ARISTOTLE

on pride as a value, I am reminded of the teachings of Aristotle. "We are what we repeatedly do. Excellence, then, is not an act, but a habit and a way of life" (Aristotle, Nicomachean Ethics, c. 350 B.C.). According to Aristotle, virtue is a moral practice which results in the gaining, maintaining and sustaining of one's values. Values are the energy force behind purposeful action. I believe my values are based on my own inner moral compass.

Growing up in a religious home and in a diverse community created conflicting views of life. My parents and elders preached to me that good or orderly behavior is self-sacrifice for the holy spirit and for the sake of imperfections on earth.

Meanwhile, no one taught me that your life belongs to you, and the good is to experience living now. Mentors and thought leaders taught me that one must learn which values to hold and how to experience them so I could live life successfully and at the same time with serenity. My challenge was to discern what standards existed for determining right behaviors as qualitatively measured through spiritual teachings. I have been taught that all moral principles must be measured against how they promote and benefit my life and happiness. Later, I discuss the effects of my spiritual teachings and what I do to maintain self-respect and a sense of pride.

I believe your values and moral standards can be transferred to you by your parents and caretakers. As infants, we absorb a lot of conscious and unconscious behaviors and attitudes. Studies have shown that prenatal and postnatal learning results support this notion. Aristotle's quote speaks to this assumption, "We are what we repeatedly do. Excellence, then, is not an act, but a habit." Furthermore, the same goes for the reverse: problems, failure, and other issues become habits, too.

With that said, let me share with you some of my reflections of how my upbringing has influenced my moral values and behaviors today. I was born during the early 50's and raised in Delaware County, Pennsylvania. I was raised in an industrial city, and it was a magnet for first and second generation immigrant families. The labor market was plentiful, and it was an economic boom period. We had one of the nation's largest shipyards, a large paper mill, steel plants, and auto and petroleum industries. We had many ethnic neighborhoods spread throughout the city. The major ethnic groups clustered together in their communities along with their plethora of churches, temples, and synagogues, as well as an equal number of saloons and social clubs. I was raised in a religious home along with my two sisters. We were close in age and enjoyed the love and attention of our parents and extended family. My parents and our elders were young and progressive and very active in our church. My father's older brother was a Baptist minister, and he had influence over my dad as his senior.

The two families lived together in a large three-story house. The rooms on the top levels were set aside for renters, and we lived in separate quarters on the main level. We enjoyed a large fenced yard that was filled with fruit trees (figs, peaches, and apples). The adults were employed with good salaries. My grand-aunt was our nanny while both my parents worked. As a young child, I was happy and living the American dream.

The adults who nurtured and raised me were proud people and well spoken. I was surrounded by music (mostly gospel) and art. In fact, we played musical instruments, sang and danced a lot. My father was the lead vocalist in his three-member group. I can remember his record album and how we would listen to him sing lead. We felt proud and unique, especially me. I believe I absorbed my father's energy and pride. Since we practically lived in the church throughout the week, we were always dressed well. As I recall, we were always smiling for the camera. At the time, attending church with my parents made me feel special and unique.

When I approached puberty, I noticed many conflicts brewing within and around me. The apparent conflict was my desire to feel accepted by my peers, the boys in the neighborhood, and, at the same time, by my parents and other elders. Although I was educated and had material things, I needed and wanted to fit in with and feel accepted by my peers, many of whom were less fortunate than I was. I began resisting what I knew was morally right. In my neighborhood, it was not "cool" to be morally and socially correct if you wished to be a member of a gang. When I found myself needing to make wise decisions and I chose not to, I felt uncomfortable afterward. My indecisive mood swings and inappropriate behaviors were confusing for those who knew me well and were familiar with my upbringing. My need to be liked by the boys in the hood was paramount; I used my allowance and my sports equipment to win their friendship. This habit continued to play out in my interpersonal relationships later in life. I continued to struggle to feel comfortable in my own skin. I allowed people, places, and things to define me and I assumed these relationships would grant me respect and acceptance.

Many years passed before I realized that I needed to look inward and learn how to get out of my own way. I began using certain principles as useful instruments to help manage and adjust my behavior and moral values, even though I continued to struggle from time to time to feel comfortable within myself. For a time, I let other people, and the drive for material things define me. I assumed these relationships would grant me respect and acceptance. Today, I deal with these matters more efficiently than in the past with the help of a few mentors and useful tools. I have discovered with the help of many others how to nurture my self-respect and self-esteem in healthier ways. This process of self-healing required me to make a decision to turn my will and my life over to the care of God on a daily basis. This decision to turn my will and life over to the trust of my Higher Power has led to a paradigm shift and a spiritual awakening.

In order to maintain self-respect and my sense of pride, I must measure my spiritual growth daily by grading my behavior and attitude using four principles. These principles are Honesty, Purity, Unselfishness, and Love. At the end of each day, I self-assess myself against each measure. This process requires me to be honest, humble and have pride.

In summary, my journey has presented me with many twists and turns. However, the foundation I received has given me the tools to recognize and take advantage of the opportunities presented to me. Having pride is a blessing that encourages me to help others achieve their goals. I consider the pride of my success to be self-acceptance.

Notes & Reflections

> "THE MAN WHO VIEWS THE WORLD AT 50 THE SAME AS HE DID AT 20 HAS WASTED 30 YEARS OF HIS LIFE."
>
> - MUHAMMAD ALI

5

Terri Freeman

Institutions Last Significantly Longer

CHAPTER FIVE

Terri Freeman

Museum Curator, Executive Director, Reginald F. Lewis Museum of Maryland African-American History and Culture, Baltimore, MD

Terri Freeman served as the President of the National Civil Rights Museum at the Lorraine Motel, in Memphis, Tennessee, where she led an international commemoration of the 50th anniversary of Dr. Martin Luther King's death. Her work in philanthropy has spanned more than 23 years, beginning with her work as the founding Executive Director of the Freddie Mac Foundation and as President of the Greater Washington Community Foundation.

Institutions Last Significantly Longer

Regarding the personal attributes I think are important for leadership, first I think it is important that leaders recognize that that is not a label you give yourself, but one which others give to you. So,

> "I BELIEVE PEOPLE COME AND GO, BUT ORGANIZATIONS AND INSTITUTIONS LAST FOR SIGNIFICANTLY LONGER IF THEY HAVE A WELL-DEFINED MISSION."

leaders require followers. Effective leaders know how to read people and situations. They understand the art of effective communication and empathy is high on their list of characteristics. For me, I learned that listening is more important than talking and that every relationship is an important and potentially useful relationship. One of the characteristics I'm most proud of is my willingness to train others and my enjoyment in training others to lead.

Providing people with direction and autonomy is very important. Leaders are willing to recognize what they don't know and share the stage with those who fill those gaps. Great leaders groom people!

I define success as a state of personal fulfillment through the work I do and the life I live. Professional success is contingent upon personal peace, clarity and fulfillment. Having led several organizations, I've always left them in good condition with an elevated organizational persona.

Success is organizational recognition. I believe people come and go, but organizations and institutions last for significantly longer if they have a well-defined mission.

Notes & Reflections

" IF THE COMMUNITY IS NOT SUCCESSFUL,
IT DOESN'T MATTER IF I AM. "

- ANGELA RYE

6

Dr. Eddie Moore, Jr.

Change is Possible

CHAPTER SIX

Dr. Eddie Moore, Jr.

Founder, The Privilege Institute (TPI), Green Bay, Wisconsin

Dr. Eddie Moore, Jr. has pursued and achieved success in academia, business, diversity, leadership and community service. In 1996, he started America & MOORE, LLC to provide comprehensive diversity, privilege and leadership training/workshops. His interview with Wisconsin Public Radio won the 2015 Wisconsin Broadcasters Association's Best Interview in Medium Market Radio, 1st Place. He is featured in the film "I'm not Racist….Am I?"

#MooreLeadership

Lesson One: Always remember to live and lead knowing that "change is possible." When your life's work is committed to fighting bias, racism, white supremacy and oppression, you must remain vigilant, courageous, strategic, and action oriented.

> "I WAKE UP EVERYDAY FEELING 'DIVINELY INSPIRED' AND FORTUNATE TO BE DOING THE WORK FOCUSED ON PURSUING PEACE, EQUITY AND JUSTICE."

Lesson Two: Always remember that "relationships matter." My leadership style has always been grounded in relationship building, lifelong learning, academic excellence, and diversity skills. I'm committed to living and leading in a multicultural society **#TogetherWeAreStronger.**

Lesson Three: Always remember I'm **#2BlessedForStress**. I'm doing the work I've been called to do. After 25+ years of longtime recovery (drugs/alcohol), my life's journey has been filled with #realchallenges and #realopportunities. I've been fortunate to evolve professionally during a time where many career paths have opened up in the areas of diversity, privilege, leadership, education and Moore. I wake up everyday feeling 'divinely inspired' and fortunate to be doing the work focused on pursuing peace, equity and justice.

Lesson Four: Be Moore #PisTaMistic. People often ask if I'm optimistic or pessimistic. My response is always "I'm neither one." Listen, don't be negative, we can always have it much worse. Additionally, it's a real privilege to believe things are getting better and not be doing anything to make them better. My suggestion is we #BeMoore #PisTaMisTic! It means: you're optimistic, but you're always taking action!

~~~

Dr. Moore is the co-founder of the online journal *Understanding and Dismantling Privilege*, co-editor of *Everyday White People Confront Racial and Social Injustice: 15 Stories, The Guide for White Women who Teach Black Boys, The Diversity Consultant Cookbook: Preparing for the Challenge* (2019) and *Teaching Beautiful Brilliant Black Girls* (2021). For 10-years, he served as Director of Diversity at Brooklyn Friends School (Brooklyn, NY) and The Bush School (Seattle, WA). Dr. Moore received his PhD from the University of Iowa in Education Leadership. His PhD research is on Black Football Players at Division III Schools in the Midwest.

Notes & Reflections

" YOU CAN'T ALWAYS EXPECT TO BE THE SMARTEST PERSON IN THE ROOM BUT YOU CAN PROMISE TO BE THE HARDEST WORKING. "

- JUDGE KETANJI BROWN JACKSON

7

Dr. Dawn D. Bennett-Alexander

Practical Diversity

CHAPTER SEVEN

Dr. Dawn D. Bennett-Alexander

Professor Emerita, Terry College of Business, University of Georgia

Dr. Bennett-Alexander is a *cum laude* graduate of the Howard University School of Law and a *magna cum laude* graduate of the Federal City College (now the University of the District of Columbia), both in Washington, D.C. She is licensed to practice law in DC and six federal jurisdictions.

My Goal

My goal was to be the best Employment Law & Legal Studies professor I could be and to help my university move forward in the area of Diversity & Inclusion. Only Whites were permitted to attend for 176 years before Blacks were admitted in 1961 and by the time I came 27 years later, the University was

> "I MEASURE MY SUCCESS BY THE HEARTS AND MINDS I TOUCHED IN WAYS THAT CREATE LASTING CHANGE THAT MAKES THE WORLD BETTER BY THE PEOPLE BEING BETTER."

still rather stuck in its pre-integration ways. I was asked to come and teach there and help move the University forward. I did that for 33 years. I also have done consulting and presentations on Employment Law & Diversity & Inclusion issues for 38 years. During that time, I have touched thousands and thousands of lives by teaching them both the law as well as life lessons that stay with them long after they leave me; they use these lessons to make the world a better place.

The characteristics needed to reach my goal

The characteristics needed to do what I did/do are an open heart that wants to make the world a better place, an absolute belief that it can happen, perseverance in the face of resistance, an iron will that does not take setbacks personally, a willingness to not be judgmental so that growth can take place, a willingness to be vulnerable and open to learning from my audience just as they learn from me, a willingness to make my principles and beliefs clear and known, a steadfast belief in myself and what I am doing, an authenticity that draws people in, and a ready, genuine smile.

What success means to me

I measure my success by the hearts and minds I touched in ways that create lasting change that makes the world better by the people being better. I also measure my success by encouraging others to be the best they can be so they can achieve things they never dreamed they could. I have thousands of communications saying that this has happened.

Plans to keep advancing myself professionally and personally

After 6 years of practicing law and 40 years of teaching, I retired effective 2/1/21, but will continue to engage in Diversity & Inclusion consulting in whatever ways present themselves. The world needs it. I created a free website (www.practicaldiversity.com) as a Diversity & Inclusion resource for the world after the 5/25/20 George Floyd killing (and many others before him) and the Amy Cooper situation in Central Park with the Harvard-educated Black male bird watcher, Christian Cooper.

My TEDTalk on Practical Diversity has been viewed over 180,000 times. I have undertaken to stretch myself into other areas of delivering D&I (Diversity & Inclusion) training, as requested, such as by being a D&I coach. I will continue to co-author my *Employment Law in Business* text, now in its 10th edition, which created the Employment Law discipline in colleges of business and has remained the industry leader since it was first first published in 1994.

I will continue to speak, advocate, and engage with the media as I have done hundreds of times over the years. And I will continue to be a ready and willing resource for those who need my input. Personally, I will continue to read, write, including writing murder mysteries with my daughter, quilt by hand to connect me to my Ancestors, garden without worrying about what else I should be doing instead, spend more time with family and engage in my other numerous hobbies.

~~~

Dr. Bennett-Alexander has garnered over 60 awards and recognitions for teaching and service, including upon her retirement in February 2021, the University of Georgia honoring her 33 years of diversity and inclusion work at UGA by establishing a new monied award for faculty significantly engaged in diversity and inclusion work, the Dawn D. Bennett-Alexander Inclusive Community Award.

Notes & Reflections

> "THERE ARE MANY THINGS I'VE LEARNED FROM STUDENTS, AND ONE THAT ALWAYS STANDS OUT TO ME WAS A LESSON THAT I LEARNED EARLY. I WAS CRITIQUING A STUDENT — I WAS IN MY 20'S THEN, AND THIS WAS A TEENAGE STUDENT — AND EVERYTHING I SAID WAS NEGATIVE. IT WAS ALWAYS, "PLAY THIS BETTER, DO THIS," AND THEN AFTER A WHILE THE STUDENT SAID, "MR. MARSALIS, COULD YOU TEACH ME FROM A POSITIVE FRAME OF REFERENCE?" AND I THINK THAT'S AFFECTED MY TEACHING MORE THAN ANYTHING. THERE'S ALWAYS THINGS YOU HAVE TO IMPROVE, BUT THERE ARE ALSO MANY THINGS THAT YOU'RE DOING WELL THAT NEED TO BE ACKNOWLEDGED. SO TO BE ABLE TO CONSTRUCT A MAP OF IMPROVEMENT THROUGH THINGS THAT ARE DONE WELL IS OFTENTIMES A MUCH BETTER METHOD OF TEACHING THAN JUST CONSTANT CRITIQUE."

- WYNTON MARSALIS

8

PHOTO CREDIT: DENNY COLLINS

Vada O'Hara Manager

The Three 'C' Principles

CHAPTER EIGHT

Vada O'Hara Manager

President & CEO, Manager Global Holdings, LLC

Vada O. is the Founder of a diversified company comprised of minority investments including hospitality, real estate, and consulting. As a member of Nike's coveted Corporate Leadership Team, Manager was assigned to join or lead teams navigating successful outcomes for supply chain/product sourcing, issue management, sports marketing and M&A transactions. He served in a similar advisory role at Levi Strauss & Company.

The Three 'C' Principles

I am not sure I have any "special sauce" for success other than these three "C" principles: continuous improvement, continuous learning and continuous working motion. The fact that I commenced this draft response after midnight (PST) on a holiday weekend is emblematic of the latter principle. As I counsel my teenage and older children – "there will always be people with seemingly greater intellect; however, the one equalizing factor you can control is your work ethic." I've long believed that certain imbalances in talent can be equalized by never being outworked to achieve success.

This is a lesson I learned early from a brick mason grandfather, a hardworking grandmother, and single mother. I was raised an only child. I worked summer jobs and also had paper routes at an early age and came to see work as rewarding and a pathway towards a better life. In high school, I joined intellectually enriching clubs such as Model UN and others that made me conversant about the world and its people and customs.

Upon arriving in Arizona for college at Arizona State University in 1979, I found even greater success through developing a reputation for working hard as a student, along with accelerating the additional component of building strong authentic relationships with classmates, university officials (including my financial officer Vince Roig – which is relevant later). Admittedly, due to both religious upbringing and witnessing past poor outcomes among friends/families related to alcohol, I surrounded myself with friends/people of similar ambition and those whose social lubricant didn't revolve around alcohol or parties.

While I enjoyed a healthy social life (and often served as a designated driver for some friends or female coeds to ensure they got home safely), I found greater use of my time by building databases of friends/people, noting personal details such as family and birthdays, to strengthen bonds

> "I WORKED SUMMER JOBS AND ALSO HAD PAPER ROUTES AT AN EARLY AGE AND CAME TO SEE WORK AS REWARDING AND A PATHWAY TOWARDS A BETTER LIFE."

between us. This is a habit that has served me well and that I continue some 40 years later – it also helps to genuinely enjoy people and to be concerned about their lives and aspirations.

Arizona Board of Regents

As mentioned, I arrived in Phoenix, Arizona in 1979 for college only knowing an uncle/aunt/cousin. In a remarkable three years – by 1982, then-Governor Bruce Babbitt (later a 1988 Presidential candidate and Interior Secretary for President Clinton) appointed me to the Arizona Board of Regents – one of the most prestigious entities in the state which governed Arizona's three universities and a large budget. I was the sole student member representing approximately 80,000 students. I was the first Black and (till now, writing in 2020) no other Blacks have served as a Regent since that time – which is actually unfortunate for the state. I was in my 20s and this is where I learned boardroom protocol and governance norms. I later joined Governor Babbitt's executive staff and served a second Governor – Rose Mofford, the state's first female leader and one of the most beloved public servants in the state's history. Her courage to appoint a young Black male as press secretary in 1988 in Arizona, the last state to recognize a Dr. MLK holiday, was ahead of its time.

PHOTO CREDIT: MARLON GLOVER, EXECUTIVE OFFICE - MAYOR

President Nelson Mandela, Washington, DC Mayor Sharon Pratt and Vada Manager

In addition, here are a few other professional highlights:

- Assisted former President Nelson Mandela in his ANC team's transition into office in South Africa
- As a former Nike exec, assisted them in business growth/ acquisitions and traveled with Michael Jordan in Asia
- Still maintain ties to my native E. St. Louis area via family/ friends in the area as well as serving on the board of Mannie Jackson Center for the Humanities at Lewis & Clark College in Edwardsville, IL.
- Serve as a corporate board director/board committee chair

for Valvoline Inc, a $4 billion global lubricants/motor oil company
- Named in 2016 & 2017 as one of SAVOY Magazine's Power 300 - Most Influential Black Corporate Directors
- Serve on the Helios Education Foundation Board – this nearly $1 billion entity was founded by my former financial officer Vince Roig who I mentioned above – little did I know he would ask me to join the board some 40 years after he invested in me through an initial Pell grant and part-time work-study job. This is emblematic of the relationship-building during my collegiate life. Although not yet open, we just opened a new campus HQ building and seeing my name on the wall of directors gives me immense pride.
- Chaired an advisory board at the US Military Academy at West Point – although I am not a grad or former military; they wanted smart outside thinkers to assist them with branding and issues.
- Our consulting business just assisted the launch of HBO MAX's lead documentary film – ON THE RECORD regarding a dark period of Def Jam Records that wasn't well known.
- Currently run several businesses via our holding company, Manager Global Holdings – our newest venture, Think TRUE just announced that we would form a consultancy that will serve Nike, JPMORGANCHASE and Facebook clients.

Three other useful principles I developed in my career and further refined while at Nike — the largest sports company in the world:

1. Stay diversified in your skills and income streams — no one is indispensable; therefore, having outcome income such as investments, a board seat or passive income provides security to perform your day job well.

2. Practice "anticipatory management" — try to see what long term trends may impact you, your career, your company and/or family. This makes you invaluable to your company and team if you are always looking at trends and ways to improve/gain market share.

3. In order to ensure you are in the loop and not held responsible for the misjudgment of others, try to be present and have a seat at the table. Every employer or partner knows my rule: "I do not publicly defend what I didn't help to define."

Finally, having had the privilege of traveling to South Africa in the 1990s and to play a small role in the transition planning in concert with the post-apartheid era of iconic President Nelson Mandela, I gleaned many useful leadership/success lessons from him.

Two such principles from his leadership style that I also deploy today are:

1) a predisposition towards "seeing the good in people" even if at times you are disappointed or even betrayed.

Next,

2) "Knowing your Rivals" is crucial for similar reasons. My brief few interactions with Nelson Mandela fundamentally shaped nearly every aspect of my worldview. His capacity for forgiveness, reconciliation and endurance of being imprisoned for 27 years are unparalleled examples of leadership and self-discipline.

Notes & Reflections

> " WE DELIGHT IN THE BEAUTY OF THE BUTTERFLY,
> BUT RARELY ADMIT THE CHANGES IT HAS GONE THROUGH TO ACHIEVE
> THAT BEAUTY. "
>
> - DR. MAYA ANGELOU

9

Cornelia Shipley

Be Clear about WHAT and HOW

CHAPTER NINE

Cornelia Shipley, BCC, PCC, ELI-MP, MBA

Founder & CEO, 3C Consulting
Powder Springs, GA

Cornelia Shipley has made her mark as an executive development consultant, strategic planning expert, and speaker. She has extensive experience in sales, sales training, and human resources.

Be Clear

My personal definition of success is to be able to be present in the moment for what matters most in that moment. At the core, people who have achieved a significant amount of professional success have taken a few critical actions.

1. They are clear about WHAT they want to accomplish and open to HOW their accomplishments will unfold.

2. They are clear about what needs to be done and take consistent action.

3. They work to expand their mindset and integrate metaphysical principles.

Notes & Reflections

> " I NEVER HAD AN OCCASION TO QUESTION COLOR, THEREFORE, I ONLY SAW MYSELF AS WHAT I WAS...A HUMAN BEING. "
>
> **- SIDNEY POITIER**

10

Chancellor Gary S. May

The Power of Persistence

CHAPTER TEN

Chancellor Gary S. May

University of California, Davis, CA

After serving as dean of Georgia Tech's College of Engineering, Gary S. May became the 7th chancellor of UC Davis in 2017. He earned his master's and Ph.D. degrees in electrical engineering and computer science at UC Berkeley. May has won numerous awards for his research in computer-aided manufacturing of integrated circuits.

The Power of Persistence

When I started college, I was excited to be there. At times, though, I couldn't help but feel out of place. I'd look around the laboratories and lecture halls, and I was often the only Black person in the room. I stood out among my fellow students, professors, and research partners.

> **THROUGH MY MOTHER, I UNDERSTOOD THE IMPORTANCE OF STAYING CONFIDENT, FOCUSED, AND STRONG.**

It may have been tempting to wonder whether electrical engineering was really the right path for me. It's not easy to feel different or apart from others. Whenever these thoughts crossed my mind, I thought about my mother and her tremendous persistence.

My mother was a groundbreaker as one of the first students to integrate the University of Missouri. It wasn't easy, especially as Jim Crow laws were still enforcing racial segregation around the country. She endured hateful language and ugly incidents that were meant to intimidate her. Despite the sometimes-tense environment she was in, she never gave up. She wasn't going to let anyone prevent her from earning a college degree. She continued to push through the negativity and studied hard, earning her diploma and starting a cherished career as a public school teacher.

I learned to persist as well. Through my mother, I understood the importance of staying confident, focused, and strong. I found a community that welcomed me and encouraged me. I found mentors who saw my potential and helped point me in the right direction if I didn't see it clearly for myself. If I saw an opportunity to help form a stronger connection with others in my field, speak out against injustice, or mentor others, I stepped forward.

I encourage everyone, especially the students I encounter, to do the same. Keep pushing, stay positive, and find others who can inspire and lift you in challenging times. The rewards of your persistence await, and even better, you can make a difference in the lives of others and in the global community.

Notes & Reflections

> " SOMEBODY HAS TO STAND WHEN OTHER PEOPLE ARE SITTING. SOMEBODY HAS TO SPEAK WHEN OTHER PEOPLE ARE QUIET. "
>
> - BRYAN STEVENSON

11

Judge Paulette R. Irons

You can do it.

CHAPTER ELEVEN

Hon. Paulette R. Irons

Judge, New Orleans, Louisiana

Judge Paulette Riley Irons serves as a New Orleans civil district court judge. She represented New Orleans District 4 in the Louisiana State Senate for 12 years. Prior to that she had served in the Louisiana House of Representatives between 1992 and 1994.

Faith in God

I am not sure my experience is one that will be glamorous or embracing but it is my recipe.

Notwithstanding hard work, I must say that my Faith in God has to be the foremost important aspect in achieving success. Being in touch with your spiritual self. This has assisted me in knowing what gives me pleasure and discovering that it comes easy. I have always wanted to

> "MY DESIRE IS TO INFORM YOUNG PEOPLE OF THE IMPORTANCE OF THEIR VOICES AND THEIR VOTES, AND THE NEED FOR THEM IN THIS STRANGE WORLD."

speak for or help people who are less fortunate.

Too often children and poor women are overlooked and their interests are not taken seriously. In my world of Politics, MONEY and VOTES are the essential ingredients in getting elected. Well, children don't have money or votes.

I believe you must listen to the positive voice that says "you can do it." All things are possible with God. The naysayers are plentiful and LOUD. They say "you will never be nothing. You will never amount to anything." If you only hear these comments, you will believe this or doubt the power of the Almighty.

Work hard and never think more highly of yourself. What we do for the least of them, we do unto GOD.

I have been in politics nearly 30 years. I do not intend to seek another elected position. My desire is to inform young people of the importance of their Voices and their VOTES, and the need for them in this strange world.

Perhaps, I'll teach. It is my belief that I may still have something to offer. It will take some additional quiet time to determine the next path I must journey.

Often you will be criticized because you could obtain more lucrative opportunities, but my life has not been lacking in any area. I believe that GOD will supply all my needs and even some of my desires if I am willing to follow his directions. After all, he is omniscient.

Notes & Reflections

> **"I KNOW IT SEEMS LIKE A LOT. BUT I REALLY ONLY DO ONE THING. I READ BOOKS. I TEACH BOOKS. I WRITE BOOKS. I THINK ABOUT BOOKS. IT'S ONE JOB."**
>
> **- TONI MORRISON**

12

Kevin Wayne Johnson

A Changed Life

CHAPTER TWELVE

Kevin Wayne Johnson

Founder & Chief Executive Officer - The Johnson Leadership Group, LLC

Kevin Wayne Johnson is a native of Richmond, Virginia, where he attended the Richmond Public School system and Virginia Commonwealth University's School of Business, earning a Bachelor of Science degree in Business Administration & Management. He retired from a 34-year career with the federal government in 2017, as a mid-level and senior-level leader, where he led small, mid-sized and large organizations. He is the author of *Leadership with a Servant's Heart*.

A Changed Life and Potential Realized

This is a brief story of support from my favorite teacher from elementary, middle, and high school. Her name is Mrs. Adkins. As a show of respect, and the way that I was raised, I never called her by her first name – Ellen. She was my eleventh grade English

> "MY LIFE'S MISSION IS TO CREATE LEADERS OF EXCELLENCE AT ALL LEVELS. IN DOING SO, BETTER LEADERS HELP TO MAKE THIS WORLD A MUCH BETTER PLACE."

teacher at Armstrong High School in my hometown of Richmond, Virginia. One day in class, during the first semester of my junior year, Mrs. Adkins' inspirational message of support, encouragement, and advocacy impacted and influenced my life. It was a memorable action on her part that I continue to pay forward as often as I can. It literally changed my life.

Immediately following my dad's retirement from the United States Marine Corps, after a twenty-year career as an enlisted soldier and commissioned junior officer, my family relocated from Virginia Beach, Virginia, to return home to Richmond. My family was accustomed to frequent moves because of dad's occupation. As a young boy, frequent moves were not very disruptive and I was able to handle the change in environment, neighborhoods, and schools alongside my mom and younger brother, Eric. However, I noticed a shift in emotions as I transitioned into middle and high school. For the first time, as I was suddenly uprooted from a familiar and comfortable surrounding, it mattered!

I attended Floyd E. Kellam High School in Virginia Beach as a freshman and sophomore in the mid-1970s. During these two phenomenally fun and exciting years of growth, development, maturing, dating, sports, and new friendships, I was excelling academically and athletically. I earned positions on the junior varsity (JV) wrestling and football teams. I wrestled at the 105-pound weight class and started on the football team as one of the three wide receivers. I wore number '88' as I attempted to emulate my favorite professional football player at the time — Lynn Swann of the Pittsburgh Steelers. Our school colors at Kellam were black and gold, just like the Steelers. Our JV wrestling and football teams were competitive, and the coaching staff was excellent. They taught us about the keys to the game as well as life lessons. I knew I wanted to continue to compete and represent my school. My teammates and I were learning valuable life skills that would sustain us through high school, prepare us for college, and ultimately, into the workplace.

At the conclusion of my sophomore year, my dad officially retired during a beautiful military ceremony in Norfolk, Virginia, at the Naval Air Station on a sunny afternoon. Soon thereafter, he notified our family during one of our weekly meetings that we would be moving back home to Richmond. While I understood and cherished the thought of being in the daily company of my grandparents, aunts, uncles, and cousins, I was devastated by the timing. Leaving my neighborhood and high school friends was heartfelt. Nevertheless, I respected dad's decision and we spent many days that summer packing and preparing to relocate. Saying goodbye was hard. Tears did flow.

The following school year came quickly. During the month of August, leading up to the start of the new semester in September, my dad enrolled me at Armstrong High School located on the east end of the city in an area known as 'Church Hill.' Under the leadership of Dr. Lucille Brown, Principal, I had a wonderful experience at this school even though my start was a bit rocky. Having a desire to continue my success on the athletic field, I attended tryouts for the varsity basketball team. Although I did not earn a position on the basketball team at Kellam High School in Virginia Beach, I did play a lot on the area playgrounds and was competitive enough to play on an organized team — so I thought. I was an all-star in little league as well as at the middle school levels. As a young sixteen-year-old, I was not aware that the varsity basketball team at Armstrong had already started their practice sessions, that the coaching staff was already familiar with their team of players, and that since the official season begins in October each year, the roster had already been selected. I learned this much later as I inquired about the selection process. However, tryouts were held but only as a formality to see what talent may be available for the following season. I did not earn a position on the varsity basketball team. I and three others were notified by the coaching staff in a most embarrassing way. They posted our names on a chart in the locker room for everyone to see.

During our English 101 class, Mrs. Adkins noticed a change in my demeanor and posture. In her eyes, I was one of her students who excelled in the subject matter, was always in good spirits, and exhibited a mild-mannered disposition. When she saw a different version of Kevin Johnson, she inquired. I informed her that I did not earn a position on the varsity basketball team and how I felt as a result. While she stated that she understood how this may make me feel, she offered a potential solution to ease the pain. Mrs. Adkins had mentioned several times in the past that I was an excellent speaker and a model student. She recommended that I talk to the varsity basketball coach about announcing the basketball games during the upcoming season. This would avail the opportunity to introduce the players, lead the play-by-play action on the court from behind the microphone so that hundreds of spectators could hear my voice. It sounded like a great idea, so I did. The coach said yes! The previous announcer had graduated the previous year and the position was vacant. [I discovered later that Mrs. Adkins was well aware of the situation and had lobbied on my behalf!] It was a great basketball season. During this same time, Mrs. Adkins also suggested that I have the same conversation with the varsity football coach. I could potentially become the football announcer from the much larger venue — the city's football stadium — where thousands of spectators, not just hundreds, would hear my voice during our home games at half time, for homecoming, and the like. I did. The football coach said yes! It was during these experiences as a junior and senior at Armstrong that I discovered my voice. That led to speaking assignments that have helped to enhance my career. I have been speaking publicly ever since, as a paid keynote speaker, Pastor, panelist, leading workshops, and the like.

Mrs. Adkins' kind display of support changed my life in the following ways:
- I discovered that I am responsible to help others in their time of need.
- I was born with a specific purpose (mission) that aligns with God's plan (vision) for my life.
- Choices are long-lasting and life-changing. Let's give others within our sphere of influence opportunities to choose their next steps over and beyond their limited options.

My life's mission is to create leaders of excellence at all levels. In doing so, better leaders help to make this world a much better place.

Notes & Reflections

" THERE ARE ALWAYS BLESSINGS THAT WE CAN FIND IN THE BURDENS WE BEAR. "

- JUDGE LAUREN LAKE

13

Dr. Alicia McGeachy

Take Stock of Myself

CHAPTER THIRTEEN

Dr. Alicia McGeachy

Postdoctoral Research Fellow at NU-ACCESS - Northwestern University, Chicago, IL

Dr. Alicia McGeachy works with an interdisciplinary, collaborative team of scientists, specialists, conservators, and curators to bridge the fields of art and science. She previously held a position as an Andrew W. Mellon postdoctoral fellow in the Department of Scientific Research at The Metropolitan Museum of Art (2018-2020). Alicia is interested in making science more equitable and accessible and has supported her scientific research with initiatives in scientific communication and outreach.

What Success Means to Me

I should start with what success means to me before going into what I think makes people successful. Success for me is progressive and is often an ever-

> "I CELEBRATE THE INCREMENTAL CHANGES AND ACCOMPLISHMENTS THAT I GARNER IN MY PURSUIT OF A GRANDER GOAL OR OBJECTIVE, WHICH HELPS ME TO STAY MOTIVATED AND READY TO TAKE ON THE NEXT CHALLENGE."

moving, ever-evolving target. For me, I feel that I have been successful when I can stop and take stock of myself and feel proud of the things that I have accomplished while setting the next goal to move me forward in life.

Success does not always look clean, or linear, and this occasionally wayward journey often makes for even better opportunities to identify and develop strengths and fortify your foundation. My ultimate goal, both professionally and personally, is to inspire and encourage others to believe that they can do it, whatever "it" means to them.

I have a particular interest in making STEM (science, technology, engineering, and mathematics) more accessible and equitable and have committed myself to seeking out opportunities to speak not only to those following behind me but also to those acting as the gatekeepers. I am pursuing a career as a cultural heritage scientist and am hoping to secure a long-term contract or permanent position that would allow me to continue to do exciting science, expand my technical and art history and materials knowledge, and to engage with others at the particularly interesting intersection of art/history and chemistry.

Some of the qualities that have helped me to be successful are being my authentic self, taking chances despite my fears and hesitations, and admitting when I do not know. I celebrate the incremental changes and accomplishments that I garner in my pursuit of a grander goal or objective, which helps me to stay motivated and ready to take on the next challenge.

In moments where I lose sight of the objective or feel overwhelmed, I make a list of what needs to be done for me to achieve the final goal. This is a classic method for making something that seems impossible, more manageable and this strategy was incredibly important to me in the middle of my PhD.

Notes & Reflections

> "I HAVE LEARNED THAT SUCCESS IS TO BE MEASURED NOT SO MUCH BY THE POSITION THAT ONE HAS REACHED IN LIFE AS BY THE OBSTACLES WHICH HE HAS OVERCOME WHILE TRYING TO SUCCEED."

- BOOKER T. WASHINGTON

14

Ambassador Delano Lewis

Know Your 'End Game'

CHAPTER FOURTEEN

Ambassador Delano Lewis

Attorney, Businessman, & Diplomat

Ambassador Lewis is currently the Chairman of Lewis Limited Productions, LLC, a global Business Development, Marketing and Management solutions consulting firm that provides high-level innovative solutions for its government and commercial clients. Ambassador Lewis heads up the Cultural Diversity & Inclusion practice.

Self-Confidence: The First Order of Business

First, in order to succeed in anything you do, whether it is in work, sports, or business, you must have self-confidence! You must believe in yourself!

The first order of business is the self-confidence to succeed. I firmly believe that self-confidence comes with

> "WITH A SUPPORTIVE FAMILY, A BELIEF IN GOD, I DID ACHIEVE SOME MEASURE OF SUCCESS. THE TRUE MEASURE WILL BE DETERMINED BY THE LEGACY THAT I LEAVE BEHIND!"

a self assessment of your strengths and weaknesses. What do I do well? What are my strengths? What are those things that I don't do so well? With this assessment I certainly can improve. You must capitalize on your strengths and then develop a game plan to make those strengths work for you!

The next order of business is a "game plan" of action. This plan embodies goals and objectives on how to achieve your plan. I suggest you begin with the "end game."

What is your ultimate goal? Where would I like to be in the next 5 to 10 years – my end game! Then you work backwards and determine what steps are needed to reach that "end game." This may include more skills training, more job or related experiences, more teambuilding and productivity. It might involve "taking some risks" and possibly moving out of your comfort zone! It will take hard work, discipline, and perseverance to reach your desired result – your end game!

Finally, your success will be enhanced if you have allies, supporters, and mentors along the way. Most leaders need teams to assist them; critical allies and those who champion you and your talents. Your success will, in most instances, depend on others — whether it is your colleagues, your team members or your mentors.

In closing, I knew early in life what my "end game" was to be! As a 17-year-old high school graduate I wanted to become a lawyer! My plan was to use the legal system to right the wrongs in our society, particularly those laws, those mores, those customs that discriminated against minorities in our society.

I did that self assessment early in life and pursued that game plan from high school, to college, to law school. Upon graduation, I pursued a government career that did assist in helping others, but also strengthened my abilities as a leader and manager in the United States and in Africa.

I spent 21 years learning the world of business in telecommunications. With the help of mentors, a strong sense of self, and perseverance, I rose from a public affairs manager to president of a subsidiary of the company.

Along the way, I was recruited to become President of National Public Radio, a public broadcasting entity. Later, I was nominated by President Bill Clinton and confirmed by the United States Senate to be the United States Ambassador to South Africa.

In summary, it was thanks to my belief in self and my relentless pursuit of my end game that I was able to succeed in life. I had the strong support of my Mother & Father and a loving spouse, children and grandchildren, that gave me the inspiration to persevere through many trials and tribulations along the journey. With a supportive family, a belief in God, I did achieve some measure of success. The true measure will be determined by the legacy that I leave behind!

~~~

Delano E. Lewis, Sr., a native Kansan, received a Bachelor's Degree from the University of Kansas in 1960 and a Juris Doctorate Degree from Washburn University School of Law, Topeka, Kansas, in 1963. Mr. Lewis served ten years in the Federal Government from 1963 until 1973. He served as an attorney with the Dept. of Justice; as an attorney in the Office of Compliance in the Equal Employment Opportunity Commission; Associate Director of the US Peace Corps in Nigeria and Country Director of US Peace Corps in Uganda, among others. In 2021, Ambassador Lewis was appointed a visiting senior fellow for Global Affairs at New Mexico State University to share his knowledge and experience in global affairs through lectures, the hosting of conferences, seminars, and workshops.

Notes & Reflections

> "SOMEONE RECENTLY SAID TO ME, "OH, YOU JUST SEEM PERFECT." AND I'M LIKE, "I'M ACTUALLY IMPERFECT, AND THAT'S WHAT MAKES ME AMAZING." I THINK THAT WAS THE MOMENT THAT ILLUMINATED FOR ME THAT I DON'T HAVE TO BE THE PICTURE-PERFECT IMAGE. I HAVE TO BE THE REAL IMAGE OF WHO I AM."

- AMANDA GORMAN

Estella Neizer-Ashun

My 5 a.m. Prayer

CHAPTER FIFTEEN

Estella Neizer-Ashun

Vice President & Chief Nursing Officer University of Cincinatti Health, Ohio

Estella Niezer-Ashun, DNPc, MN, BSN, RN, CPHQ, has more than 15 years of nursing leadership experience in the health care industry. Her expertise includes inpatient nursing services, employee engagement, quality and risk management, compliance, peri-operative and procedural services, hospital operations, long-term acute care (LTAC), rehabilitation, and community health.

My 5 a.m. Prayer

My spirituality and relationship with God has played a huge role in my life personally and professionally. The Bible is a book that I have looked up to for advice on life, quality traits and habits to be successful in life as it contains a lot of great nuggets for life and especially for those in leadership. As a young girl, my father always woke me up daily at 4 a.m. to pray before I started my day. This is a habit that I have continued throughout my life. I wake up daily at 5 a.m. to pray and meditate before starting my day.

> "I STRONGLY BELIEVE THAT KNOWING AND UNDERSTANDING YOUR PURPOSE WILL FUEL YOUR SUCCESS IN LIFE."

I am a firm believer that every experience in life, good or bad, is an important contributory factor for our growth.

There are no good or bad experiences. They are all opportunities for learning and growth. A quest for wisdom, coupled with the willingness to persevere, is an important character trait to help you achieve your goals. Perseverance is key, especially in our current environment where things seem to be moving at the speed of light and the tendency is to move on after the first try.

Success to me occurs when you become knowledgeable of your unique purpose and calling in life and master the ability to use it for the benefit of others.

I believe that for continued personal and professional growth you have to commit to becoming a lifelong learner. This involves continuing to keep abreast of new research in your area of expertise. Professionally, I am working on my doctorate degree. Moreover, I subscribe to various publications of professional organizations relevant to my current profession.

On a personal level, I also work on my spiritual growth, which allows me to become centered to know my purpose and to help me walk in that purpose.

To reiterate my prior comment, I strongly believe that knowing and understanding your purpose will fuel your success in life.

Notes & Reflections

> "AS YOU ACHIEVE, YOU TEACH. AS YOU LEARN AND GROW, YOU IMPART THAT WISDOM."
>
> **- KESHIA KNIGHT PULLIAM**

16

Ogbonna Hagins

Maximize Life

CHAPTER SIXTEEN

Ogbonna Hagins

Publisher (Philly Word Magazine) & Educator (Architecture)

Ogbonna Hagins, "Philly Green Man, Environmental Superhero," in a former life, worked for architectural firms (for four years) and taught architecture for nine years at Dobbins High School, Philadelphia. In 2008, inspired by the presidential candidacy of Barack Obama and increasing knowledge of the green economy, he decided to devote himself to making a difference in solving some of the problems with the environment.

Maximize Life

Success is when you maximize the life that you have been given to the absolute fullest.

As a teacher of Architecture and Design, at the Murrell Dobbins High School in Philadelphia, I achieved success by providing real life lessons intertwined with the architecture class.

Being real. Being true. Being authentic is one way that I achieved success.

Success, in the end, is the ability to effect positive change in oneself in order to provide positive change in others.

Why is there a need for change?
Ultimately, one will change whether they consciously do it or not. It's best to be able to do it consciously. To be successful, you must be willing to change.

I retired from teaching after 9 years. This was done for the specific reason to make sure that my twin boys, who were yet to be born, would be successful. By staying home, contrary to what many thought, I was able to excel even more. But most importantly, I was able to instill lessons in my children from birth.

Sacrificing one's self, sacrificing immediate gratification and sacrificing things, will allow one to achieve success. It's all about the information that you absorb or accumulate through studying and reading.

In today's age where information is at your fingertips, there is no reason for Success not to abound.

Surrounding yourself with people who are positive and forward-thinking and in a position to connect you with more people who are successful is key. Success tends to breed success and one should befriend those who are successful.

> "IN TODAY'S AGE WHERE INFORMATION IS AT YOUR FINGERTIPS, THERE IS NO REASON FOR SUCCESS NOT TO ABOUND."

The question is: What exactly is success? For most, success is measured by how much money one has. And I guess on a certain level that is success. For me, I have had success on many levels. None of those successful Endeavors revolved around making money. I have many areas in which I have experienced success.

Ogbonna Hagins, Candidate for City Council of Philadelphia, 2019

The following are what I consider my major successes.

1. Teaching — I was a success at teaching, because it was all about imparting information to the students who were entrusted to me. I had to determine by trial and error what would be the best way to make them respond.

Ultimately, it was because of respect. As students and as individuals who have their own ways of learning, I developed their respect by immersing myself in Hip-Hop culture, which was what the majority of the students were into whether through the music, style of dress or communication styles. I ended up motivating them to believe in themselves and their abilities. Because of this, many of my students participated in major competitions and placed first. Three notable Awards my students won were in the General Building Contractors Association model building competition. The students had to design a baseball stadium to house 45,000 people.

I was a success, because I motivated and inspired my students to be a success.

2. Publishing — As publisher of Philly Word Magazine, a hip hop themed magazine that was founded in 1999, the ultimate goal was/is to Educate, Empower and Entertain. During the four years that we continuously published, we were on the frontline of breaking many artists and again, looking to the benefit of the masses. We did this by providing an outlet for those artists and activists and writers to develop their craft and to be successful. In fact, we were the first publication to feature the rap artists Eve, Beanie Sigel, and many others. We also featured writers such as Pulitzer Prize winner Trymaine Lee, Chuck Creekmore, Bobby Booker and many others.

3. Recycling — With former president Barack Obama encouraging Americans to engage in the green economy, I began recycling and gathering the discarded usable items that are thrown away daily in America, and in particular, Philadelphia. I've been able to recover tens of thousands of usable sneakers, shoes, electronics, clothing, and anything else you can think of that people buy regularly. My idea again was to be able to make the well-being of others my number one priority, as well as contribute to a society that is sustainable and environmentally friendly. Over the last 12 years that I have been curating these usable Goods, I have been responsible for more than 1 million pairs of Footwear being distributed to West Africa and Haiti.

Ogbonna Hagins and son, Anu, a talented artist

So, ultimately as you can see, success for me always came from giving. My grandmother and her religious belief would always say the more you give, the more God will give back to you. In every single case where I chose to look at what I needed to do to better the well-being of others, I achieved success. Many have been the beneficiaries of all my activities. Thus, success is contributing to others' success.

Notes & Reflections

> "THERE ARE TWO QUESTIONS THAT WE HAVE TO ASK OURSELVES. THE FIRST IS "WHERE AM I GOING?" AND THE SECOND IS "WHO WILL GO WITH ME?""
>
> **- HOWARD THURMAN**

17

Queen Mother Falaka Fattah

God's Eye Perspective

CHAPTER SEVENTEEN

Queen Mother Falaka Fattah

Co-Founder, House of Umoja, Philadelphia, PA

Queen Mother Falaka Fattah was born Frances Ellen Brown in Philadelphia, Pennsylvania. After graduating from South Philadelphia High School for Girls, she studied writing at Temple University, Philadelphia. Along with her husband, David Fattah, Sister Fattah founded the House of UMOJA as a publishing company in 1968 and welcomed delinquent youths into her family in 1969. She has received over 100 national and local awards for community service and journalism.

God's Eye Perspective

My mother, a former teacher, gave me a book *One Hundred Great Lives*.

Within the book is a chapter on Mahatma Gandhi...my favorite. Reflecting, I think his Life influenced my God's eye perspective.

> "...ACCEPT LIFE'S CHALLENGES AND DIFFICULTIES, WHILE LEARNING FROM MISTAKES."

In 1994, Dr. Arun Gandhi, grandson of Mahatma Gandhi, asked me to write a poem for the book, *World without Violence*. I wrote the following:

"A New World"

For our future world without violence, cooperation replaces competition and love replaces oppression. For our future world without violence, all religions and all nations melt into one nation. As inhabitants of this brave new world, I am you and you are me and we are one together. And in the final analysis, perhaps, the activity of the research for this nonviolent world embodies "our essential worship of God."

This was my spiritual NobLesse Oblique (Noble Obligation). However, when a friend (who was almost a second father to me) asked me to help him write a book, I failed him. He explained that he had a recurring dream, in which he saw the bodies of Black youth surrounding the William Penn statue. He thought we must save them and asked me to record his thoughts. I agreed, but procrastinated. When questioned about the delay, I explained that because of bills, I had to work on other jobs. His response was to pay off all my bills.

Overjoyed, I celebrated by taking my children on a picnic. Within days my friend died of a sudden heart attack. The guilt and shock of his passing was devastating. That obligation, not being met, changed my direction. It was a horrible mistake. Lesson learned was that obligation means that your word is your bond.

Thus, my advice to today's youth is to accept Life's challenges and difficulties, while learning from mistakes.

Be sincere/passionate in reaching for your objectives and goals. Be loyal and patient with yourself and others. Be also humble, compassionate, and generous with your time when attempting to help others.

During difficult times, focus on being an active listener to better understand their situation. Finally, on your Life's journey, take the long view, and be grateful for your blessings. You are indeed God's masterpiece.

I found success when a former troubled teenager (who used to live in my home) returned to visit as a man. To my joy, he presented as a loving husband, proud father, and productive citizen.

Determination has been the most instrumental in the achievement of my goals, both personally and professionally. In the twilight of my years, I continue to focus on solution-based activities geared to the pursuit of nonviolence.

This lifelong pursuit continues out of a sense of love and duty and obligation.

~~~

Queen Mother Falaka Fattah's work has been praised by two United States Presidents, Jimmy Carter and Ronald Reagan.

On December 28, 2011, Queen Mother Falaka Fattah was honored by the Philadelphia City Council at the Mayor's Reception Room for having used House of Umoja to transform the lives of gang members. As the Philadelphia Tribune reported, "During her birthday celebration, Fattah was lauded for impacting the lives of more than 3,000 young men who, at various points, lived at the house, located in the 1400 block of Frazier Street."

Notes & Reflections

> " I EAT 'NO' FOR BREAKFAST. [I HAVE] BEEN TOLD MANY TIMES DURING MY CAREER THINGS FROM 'YOU ARE TOO YOUNG, IT'S NOT YOUR TURN, THEY ARE NOT READY FOR YOU, NO ONE LIKE YOU HAS DONE IT BEFORE.' I HAVE HEARD ALL OF THOSE THINGS MANY TIMES OVER THE COURSE OF MY CAREER, BUT I DIDN'T LISTEN. "

- VICE PRESIDENT KAMALA HARRIS

18

Dr. H. Leslie Adams

Focus on Broader Goals

CHAPTER EIGHTEEN

Dr. H. Leslie Adams

Composer, Composer in Residence Creative Arts, Inc., Cleveland, Ohio

Dr. Adams is the composer of the music drama, "Blake." He has worked in all media, including symphony, ballet, choral, vocal solo, and keyboard. Adams' works have been performed by the Prague Radio Symphony, Iceland Symphony, Buffalo Philharmonic, Indianapolis Symphony and New York City Opera. Adams earned degrees from Oberlin College (Conservatory of Music), Long Beach State University, and Ohio State University.

Focus on Broader Goals

As time goes on I have relaxed my character traits and habits to focus on broader goals rather than shorter range traits.

I have consciously sought professional and social asso-

> "...DEDICATION TO MY WORK, MAINTAINING THE HIGHEST STANDARDS POSSIBLE, AND FINDING TIME TO RELAX MY MIND, SPIRIT, AND BODY."

ciates that have a relaxed approach to their personal lives and careers. In this regard, I note there are fewer people in my life with traits similar to my own: dedication to my work, maintaining the highest standards possible, and finding time to relax my mind, spirit, and body.

Regarding the last, I walk thirty minutes every day without taking a break, and maintain a well-rounded diet of fruits, vegetables, some carbohydrates and a little fish and meat.

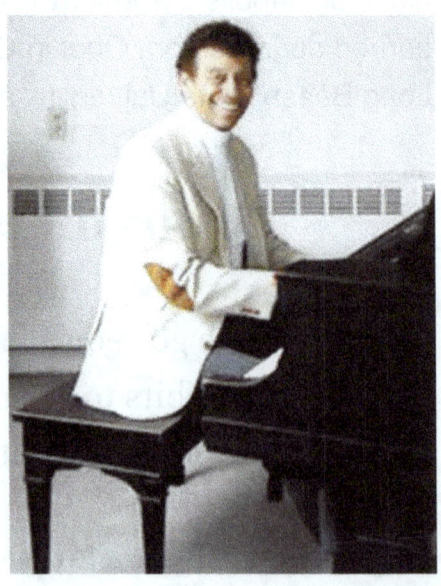

Notes & Reflections

> "OUR LIVES BEGIN TO END THE DAY WE BECOME SILENT ABOUT THINGS THAT MATTER."
>
> - DR. MARTIN LUTHER KING, JR.

Dr. Ellen Grant

Servant Leadership

CHAPTER NINETEEN

Dr. Ellen Grant, PhD, LCSW-R

Deputy Mayor, Buffalo, New York

Dr. Grant has over 25 years in health, behavioral health, education and human services. Her past leadership positions include Fellow, *Say Yes to Education* National Office; Commissioner, Erie County Department of Mental Health; CEO, Niagara Falls Memorial Medical Center. She has taught at the undergraduate and graduate levels in college & university positions (State University of New York at Buffalo, D'Youville College). She is also a licensed clinical social worker and executive coach. Ellen's first book, *Managing in Black & White*, was originally published in 1991. She also authored a chapter in the book, *Go Tell Michelle: African American Women Write to the First Lady.*

Four P's of Leadership

1. Perseverance — Act like you're powerful and powerful things will happen for you. Stay focused on your own goals without comparing yourself to others. One failed act does not doom the entire project; each day is another opportunity to begin anew.

2. Piety — A belief in a higher power other than yourself, however you believe and or practice.

3. Principles — What do you value and draw the line at? I left a well-paid position once because I did not agree with the objective the governance structure had in mind.

4. Positive use of Power — Use it wisely to help, elevate others. Success to me is who have I helped? Have I done my best? Am I still striving and setting goals for myself? What does the next two years look like for Ellen?

> "SUCCESS TO ME IS WHO HAVE I HELPED? HAVE I DONE MY BEST? AM I STILL STRIVING AND SETTING GOALS FOR MYSELF? WHAT DOES THE NEXT TWO YEARS LOOK LIKE FOR ELLEN?"

~~~

Dr. Grant's 2017 publication is *Management for You: Leadership Can Be Colorblind.* More recently, January 2021, she published *The Female Worker's Fourteen Commandments for Powering Up your Career.*

Ellen has received a number of awards at the local and state levels, including Western New York Women's Hall of Fame. Ellen is Past President, NY State, National Association of Social Workers. She currently serves on the Administration & Supervision Committee, National. Ellen is also the recipient of an Honorary Doctorate from Medaille College in 1992. In 1996, Ellen was elected, President, NY State Association of Counties, the second woman and first Black in the association's 72-year history. In 1997, The International Women's Forum Leadership Foundation selected her as one of 12 women internationally to participate in a yearlong leadership training program that included training at Harvard University. Her voluntary work includes emeritus status on the State University of NY at Buffalo Foundation, WNY Women's Foundation, Trocaire College. She continues to serve on the Advisory Board, the Black Women's Health Study, Boston University, the largest health research study of its kind in the US.

Notes & Reflections

> "I HAVE LEARNED OVER THE YEARS THAT WHEN ONE'S MIND IS MADE UP, THIS DIMINISHES FEAR; KNOWING WHAT MUST BE DONE DOES AWAY WITH FEAR."
>
> **- ROSA PARKS**

20

Rejji P. Hayes

Competence, Work ethic, and Integrity

CHAPTER TWENTY

Rejji P. Hayes

Executive Vice President & Chief Financial Officer, CMS Energy and Consumers Energy, Jackson, MI

Rejji P. Hayes is executive vice president and chief financial officer of CMS Energy and its principal subsidiary, Consumers Energy. He was named to this position in 2017. Hayes is responsible for treasury, tax, investor relations, accounting, financial planning & analysis, internal controls and compliance, and mergers & acquisitions. Hayes also serves as executive sponsor of the Minority Advisory Panel, one of CMS Energy's largest employee resource groups.

Environment Matters

Going back to childhood, I'm from a small town, about 30 minutes north of Boston called Andover, Massachusetts. My parents were really focu-

> "BOTH IN HIGH SCHOOL AND COLLEGE, I DIDN'T HAVE MANY RESOURCES. SO, THERE ARE CERTAIN THINGS THAT WERE A SOURCE OF STRESS, LIKE HAVING A LOT OF STUDENT LOANS."

sed on making sure that my sister and I had access to a good education, and a safe environment. And so, they actually moved from the Boston area where my dad grew up to that town, really on a wing and a prayer because, they didn't really have a great deal of money, but they knew that that area would offer my sister and me perhaps a greater opportunity than they had.

My mother's an immigrant from Barbados; my dad is from the South End Projects of Boston. So that decision that they made, before I was born, did change the course of my life because growing up in that environment, that suburb, the public schools were better than what I would've had exposure to had I grown up in Boston, where my dad grew up. There were fewer things I had to worry about from a safety perspective compared to what he experienced growing up.

Also, what was most beneficial was that I just got to see before my very eyes varying levels of success or numerous ways in which people could be successful: I'd go to friends' houses and their parents were doctors, they were lawyers, they were academics, they were in the business world. And just seeing that type of variety of success broadened my horizons and at an early age, started planting seeds of what I could potentially become. So I would say that was really beneficial to my upbringing.

Quality Education Counts
I had the good fortune to go to a good private school from the 9th grade to the 12th grade, the equivalent of high school in the US. It was a very selective and rigorous academic experience. That prepared me well and broadened

my horizons as to which colleges I thought might be within my possibilities of being admitted to. I chose a good diverse set of colleges, some large, some small, but generally all focused on the Northeastern area, which is where I lived. So, a couple of Ivy League schools, as well as smaller schools that were also highly reputable, and to be fully transparent, all the schools, offered a very good education.

I got into Cornell. I got into an Ivy League school, a very big school. I ended up with Williams College, Amherst College, Wesley University, and we deciding among those four, ultimately I went to Amherst. In addition to feeling really good about the educational opportunities at those schools, which I felt were all pretty comparable, I also played soccer, and that was a great passion of mine at that time. I liked the opportunity to have an impact on the Amherst soccer team, because they actually weren't all that good. They were bringing in a freshman class, and we could all have a big impact. Our first season where we started five first-year players, freshmen, as they say in the US, I was one of those players that played midfield and before we joined the team, they had only won one game out of about 17. And that first year, we were ranked 16th in the country, because we had a great season. We went to the NCAA (National Collegiate Athletic Association) tournament and I had an impact at a very young age; I liked the aspect of really having a big impact. So that was also what drew me to Amherst.

Dealing with Stress
Both in high school and college, I didn't have many resources. So, there are certain things that were a source of stress, like having a lot of student loans. I was constantly doing what we call work-study. I was always doing dishes; at times, I had three or four jobs. For example, I was security at one of the museums on

the campus. I never had a computer or laptop. But Amherst had good resources so there were certainly computer centers that I could utilize, but that just made it tough. There's a source of insecurity when you have a lot less resources than other people.

As I said, I played sports at Amherst. I was a soccer player, so I had friends as soon as I got on campus; I was playing with the 18 men on that team and had a lot of friends who were upper classmen because we had seniors, juniors, and sophomores. I certainly didn't lack popularity. I had a good time there. Also, there were some family matters that were just a source of distraction. So, it wasn't an easy time but I enjoyed it all the same because the education, as I mentioned, was quite good. I learned a lot there and it certainly offered a good array of opportunities when I graduated. So, I'm forever grateful for that experience.

The Years After Amherst — Before Harvard
I worked for about three years, after graduation. Most of that time was with Accenture, the consulting firm, which was at that time called Anderson Consulting. I was there for about three years and that's when I applied and got into business school. And then, there was about a six, seven-month window between when I left Accenture and then matriculated at Harvard. And in that little time between, I ended up working at a startup, which were a big rage at that time. I wanted to give it a try and also just experience something new professionally. I actually enjoyed it; there was an unstructured nature to it, and a pace to it that I found invigorating. It didn't work out, like, I didn't end up a billionaire or anything like that, but I had fun working there. And then I ended up going to Harvard for business school.

The Harvard Business School Experience
It was good; it was every bit as academically intense as people

> "...THE RECIPE I'VE TRIED TO LIVE BY IS JUST WHEREVER I'VE GONE, AND I'VE WORKED AT QUITE A FEW PLACES SINCE I GRADUATED FROM COLLEGE, IS TO VERY CONSISTENTLY EXHIBIT COMPETENCE, WORK ETHIC, AND INTEGRITY."

advertise. They really are strong advocates of the case study methodology. And so, the discussions are very fluid. You're not looking at problem sets and going through textbooks.

There's some of that in the second year but in the first year, it's basically all case studies and half of your grade is based on participation. It's not as simple as, saying, the answer is five! Most times, you're expected to give a pretty detailed and thorough synopsis of any topic you want to raise. And so that takes some getting used to, because previously, in my academic environment I'd work and I'd study and then take a test. At Harvard, giving those kinds of speeches in front of 85 other equally impressive and talented people, that took a little getting used to that first year. By the second year, I really enjoyed it — after getting through that sort of initial trial phase. But the first year was a little tough. Also, there were a lot of subjects that I hadn't gotten exposed to because I was a Russian language and literature major in college. I went to a liberal arts school, and at Accenture, I certainly got some business acumen there, but no, I wasn't an accountant; I didn't know finance. There was a lot I had to learn there. So that first year, I was very, very focused on trying to just climb the curve and also just get used to the class participation side and offering detailed substantive thoughts about these case studies.

The Harvard Study Group Experience
In the first year, it's almost a necessity, so I certainly had a study group. I think most people go that route and that's just a great way to divide and conquer because, with a bunch of cases you have to read each day, it is helpful

to have some interdependence where you can rely on somebody else to prepare notes for a case study while you do another case study. It's just a good way to work together. It also is a good way to build affinity because a lot of people are new. So that was a great way to really form good bonds.

I was in a couple of study groups and made some really good friends who I have to this day almost 20 years later.

By the second year, you become really efficient. I didn't do much in the way of study groups in that second year. I had a couple of group projects, but by the second year, you have more of an elective curriculum and you're just more efficient as a student. So, I didn't see the need for it much the second year, but first year certainly relied heavily upon that structure.

Finance: The Road to Mastery
My primary motive for going to business school was to learn accounting in a formal way. I wanted to learn finance; I wanted to know valuation theory. I got a lot of that education at Harvard and that prepared me to, at least have, a baseline or some working knowledge of accounting, finance, and valuation before going into investment banking. I thought that to make that transition as a consultant directly into the investment banking business would've been a very steep learning curve. So, I thought business school offered a very nice bridge to that experience.

Thriving in the Corporate World
The corporate world certainly has its challenges. My experience has solely or primarily been in the United States in terms of the companies I have worked for, but I've done some international business. One of the challenges if you're a minority in any way, whether it's through race, gender, or otherwise, you're general-

ly going to be a very small minority. And so, just being the only one, you get used to that as you might get through colleges as well in the US. But that offers its own unique set of challenges because, people will have preconceived notions to some extent. We've seen some of that where their expectations of you in some cases are lower. With every person you meet, you have to dispel those myths pretty quickly. And the recipe I've tried to live by is just wherever I've gone, and I've worked at quite a few places since I graduated from college, is to very consistently exhibit competence, work ethic, and integrity. If you consistently do that, you'll see that people will side with you and mentor and sponsor you. But it does take time. And again, there are some people who may never get there; there are certainly challenges. Also, what has helped me is that I did move around and the times when I moved, I always wanted to make sure that I really had a good interest in what I was doing.

I heard Kenneth Chenault say, I think in 1998, when I was at a lecture at Columbia Business School. He said that to be successful anywhere, you have to believe in the product or service that your company's offering. And the absence of that will make things very difficult. So I really tried to go to sectors and businesses that I found deeply interesting. Because if you find it interesting, well then, you're going to spend the extra time to get better at it, and then, that will give you an advantage over your peers who may not have as much passion about the subject matter. In addition to exhibiting those traits, I've also tried to make sure that wherever I've gone, I believed in what they were doing and had some passion behind it; that's what I liked about investment banking. That's what I liked about M&A, and certainly now I've been in power and energy for over 10 years and still have good passion for that business as well.

> "I DO THINK IT IS IMPORTANT TO PURSUE OPPORTUNITIES THAT YOU HAVE AN INTEREST IN. SO, AVOID FOLLOWING THE HERD FOR THINGS THAT SOUND INTERESTING OR APPEALING BECAUSE OTHER PEOPLE ARE DOING IT VERSUS WHAT DEEPLY RESONATES WITH YOU."

Serving on Corporate Boards

With every experience, you broaden your skillset and what you know. And so, I do think that, my professional experience and the time I spent in investment banking and consulting where I had access and exposure to a number of clients and sectors broadened my business acumen. And then my time in the power and energy sector, basically on the principal side, working for a publicly traded company and having natural interface with boards, because you're always seeking board approval for some business initiative or strategic decision, that certainly helped me.

And then I started on the nonprofit side with boards. I served as an alumni trustee for my alma mater, not Amherst College, but Phillips Andover Academy, that private school I went to that certainly broadened my experience, and then University of Illinois at Chicago, serving on their board of visitors, and the YMCA. And so, all of those experiences and just understanding how boards interface with management have prepared me well for now raising the stakes and joining a public company board in Fortive Corporation. They're based in Everett, Washington State, and they're an industrial technology company. One other experience I should mention is that I also Chaired the board of a bank that was a subsidiary of CMS Energy, the company I work for now; that was a very rich experience because I joined the Board in 2018 and became chair. And again, just that interface, understanding how they work, their responsibilities, whether it's audit, compensation, nominating and governance, just understanding how those committees interface with the board, the responsibilities they have, the risks they need to have oversight of. That prepared me well for joining the Fortive board and I now Chair their audit committee and serve as a member of the comp committee. I felt comfortable hitting the ground running and chiming in.

Advice for Up-and-comers

I will pass on or pay forward the advice I got — what I heard Ken Chenault say many years ago at that event at Columbia business school that I was fortunate to sit in on. I do think it is important to pursue opportunities that you have an interest in. So, avoid following the herd for things that sound interesting or appealing because other people are doing it versus what deeply resonates with you.

After business school, I started pursuing finance. That was of great interest. I was in that business for almost 10 years and then the power and energy sector has been interesting to me as well. And so, I do think it's really important to believe in the product or service your company's offering and that's what you should pursue because, again, if you're not as interested or passionate about the subject, you're not going to spend as much time dedicating yourself to perfecting your craft; that will obviously not compare you well versus your peers who are spending that extra time. So that's critically important.

Going back to my earlier comment, I do think wherever you go, it's really important to exhibit confidence, work ethic and integrity, because as somebody who now evaluates people either to potentially hire them or judge whether they should get promoted or get opportunities, that is the first thing I look for: those raw materials. If any of those aren't there, then I write people off pretty quickly, particularly integrity; if you don't have that, then, you're not going to work with me. So, I think those are some things that

I would strongly advise people who are looking for success to consider, and it doesn't have to be in just a business role. I think in any organizational pursuit, you should really have some interest in what you're doing. People say pursue your passions a lot. I'm not saying it that strongly, but definitely, pursue something that's of interest to you. And then exhibit competence, work ethic and integrity, wherever you go.

Professional Prospects
What we feel quite good about at CMS Energy and our major subsidiary, Consumers Energy, which is a regulated electric and gas utility based in Michigan, is that we are quite proud of the stand we've taken to exit our coal generation facilities by 2025 and do our share to reduce the effects of carbon emissions on climate change. That action took a lot of time and effort, to really make sure that we could not only do what's right for the planet by reducing our carbon emissions by 60% by 2025 based on 2005 levels, but make sure we can still maintain reliable electric service for the people of Michigan, because that's a lot of capacity from an electric generation perspective and making sure that we could responsibly keep the lights on while taking out all of that capacity.

It's a big effort, in also making sure our investors who plan to earn a return on those assets are still made whole. And then I would say, professionally, from an individual perspective, I always want to continue to learn and be challenged. I feel like there are certainly plenty of opportunities to continue to learn and be challenged by at CMS Energy. And with the Fortive board that I've joined, they're doing very different things than what I'm doing at CMS, and so there's a lot of growth opportunity there. I have the continued desire to broaden my skillset, learn more and then just obviously contribute to society.

Personal Prospects

From a personal perspective, I've got a seven-year old daughter named Harper and a nine-year-old named Hunter and my wife, Celeste. We've been married now for 15 years, and we're very focused on making sure we raise two responsible, ambitious, hardworking, highly principled children. Like every parent, that is a focal point and there's no guarantee. So, we're very focused on that.

Definition of Success

To me, it's very simple. I think if you can get paid to do something you enjoy that ideally contributes to society, that, to me is success. It doesn't matter how much you make, as long as you can afford to pay your rent, and then have the other things that people enjoy in life.

~~~

Hayes also serves as chairman of the board of EnerBank USA®, a CMS Energy subsidiary and nationwide provider of home improvement loans. Hayes joined CMS Energy from ITC Holdings Corp., a regulated electric transmission utility, where he began his tenure as vice president, finance and treasurer in 2012 before serving as chief financial officer from 2014 to 2016. In his role as ITC's chief financial officer, Hayes was responsible for the company's accounting, tax, mergers & acquisitions, internal audit, investor relations, treasury, financial planning and analysis, management reporting and risk management functions. He co-led the strategic review that resulted in the sale of ITC – which was then a publicly traded company – to Fortis, Inc., a leading North American utility holding company. Under Hayes' tenure as CFO, ITC's market capitalization increased from approximately $4.7 billion to $7 billion.

Notes & Reflections

> "I DON'T CARE WHO YOU ARE OR WHAT YOU DO BUT IF YOU HAVE ANY ASPIRATIONS OF BEING SUCCESSFUL, YOU'RE GOING TO HAVE TO GET UNCOMFORTABLE. BECAUSE, LET ME TELL YOU SOMETHING. IF YOU STAY IN YOUR COMFORT ZONE, THAT'S EXACTLY WHERE YOU'LL FAIL."
>
> **- STEVE HARVEY, COMEDIAN**

21

Laura Hodges

Each New Day, A New Opportunity

CHAPTER TWENTY-ONE

Laura Hodges

Designer, Laura Hodges Studio, Baltimore/Washington, DC

With a boutique interior design firm located in the Baltimore/Washington, DC area, Laura Hodges focuses on creating beautiful, tailored spaces while fully expressing every client's individual style and taste. Laura holds a bachelor's degree in business, an interior design degree from the New York School of Interior Design and LEED accreditation for practicing sustainable design. Laura's signature aesthetic is tailored and eclectic, incorporating unique vintage and antique finds, curated art and natural elements.

Each New Day, a New Opportunity

My definition of success is not bound by financial gains or acknowledgment by others, although both are definitely appreciated. I have been fortunate enough in my life to be able to find my way on

> "I FIND GREAT JOY AND SATISFACTION IN LEARNING AND GROWING BOTH PERSONALLY AND PROFESSIONALLY AND I AM ALWAYS GRATEFUL FOR THE OPPORTUNITY TO HELP OTHERS TO DO THE SAME."

my own terms, with the support of family and friends, and this freedom has allowed me to really understand my own needs and interests. To me, success is not a stopping point or a goal, it's part of the journey. Finding moments throughout each day to appreciate my life, my family and my work means that I'm able to see success as a part of every day rather than a distant goal. I've always been very aware of the brief time we might have in this world so I try to live without regrets and pursue any opportunity I have to grow and experience something new. I would rather try something and potentially fail than regret not taking an opportunity to experience something life has to offer. I try to teach others to think in this way, if they're so inclined, so that they gravitate towards positivity and a sense of curiosity.

I find great joy and satisfaction in learning and growing both personally and professionally and I am always grateful for the opportunity to help others to do the same. I think that one of my greatest strengths is an eternal sense of optimism and, at the same time, gratefulness. In this way, each new day is a new opportunity to discover and create. I'm optimistic about the outcome of any challenge but also grateful for what I already have accomplished.

~~~

Laura was featured in Traditional Home as a New Trad and House Beautiful as a Next Wave Designer. She was also named one of the top 20 Designers for 2020 by Sotheby's Home and she recently won a Luxe Red Award for best Contemporary/Modern space from Luxe Magazine. Laura is also a brand ambassador for the Sustainable Furnishings Council, which is working to increase awareness for sustainable interior design.

Notes & Reflections

> **" KNOWLEDGE MAKES A MAN UNFIT TO BE A SLAVE. "**
>
> **- FREDERICK DOUGLASS**

22

Dr. Anthony K. Wutoh

Universal Truths I Learned as a Child

CHAPTER TWENTY-TWO

Dr. Anthony K. Wutoh

Provost, Chief Academic Officer, Howard University

Dr. Anthony Wutoh received a Bachelor of Arts degree in Biochemistry from the University of Maryland, Baltimore County, in 1987. He then completed a Bachelor of Science in Pharmacy and (Pharmacoepidemiology) at the University of Maryland, Baltimore School of Pharmacy. Dr. Wutoh has led, and participated in various international programs including sponsored projects (USAID, CDC, PEPFAR, etc.) in Nigeria, South Africa, Zambia, Kenya, Rwanda, Tanzania, Ethiopia, Ghana, etc.

Universal Truths I Learned as a Child

As a young child, my parents emigrated from Ghana to the United States. From my youth, I remember various axioms and proverbs that my parents would share that continue to guide me, even today.

> **SUCCESS IN LIFE IS NOT ABOUT HOW MANY THINGS WE CAN ACQUIRE, OR HOW MUCH MATERIAL WEALTH WE CAN OBTAIN, BUT THE DIFFERENCE WE WILL MAKE IN THE LIVES OF PEOPLE THAT WE TOUCH EVERY DAY.**

"No man is an island unto himself,"

"Even a thousand years is not forever,"

"Always do your best,"

"Choose one thing, and do it well," and

"Only God knows."

As I consider difficult decisions, or face tough choices, the lessons from my childhood and voices of my parents continue to be a guiding light for me.

As my wife and I have raised our own children, I find myself repeating many of these same axioms and adages to help direct my daughters, nephews and nieces.

I have found that regardless of our culture, or where we are born, there are universal truths that will help to guide and direct us to be of greater service to one another.

Success in life is not about how many things we can acquire, or how much material wealth we can obtain, but the difference we will make in the lives of people that we touch every day.

Notes & Reflections

> "TRUST IS LOST IN BUCKETS AND GAINED IN DROPS."
>
> - JUDGE FAITH JENKINS

23

Dr. Lindsey Cameron

Fiercely Dedicated to My Path

CHAPTER TWENTY-THREE

Dr. Lindsey Cameron

Assistant Professor of Management, Wharton, University of Pennsylvania

My research focuses on how changes in the modern workplace (e.g., algorithms/machine learning, short-term employment contracts, variable pay) affect work and workers. I recently completed a five-year ethnography of the largest employer in the gig economy, the ride-hailing industry, exploring how algorithms are fundamentally reshaping the nature of managerial control and how workers navigate this new workplace.

What Success Means to Me

Being fiercely dedicated to my path. Every tradition has a different name for it — following your "dharma", *deeping* into your "odu", living your "best life" — yet they ultimately all mean the same thing. First ask yourself, What is the unique work that only you can do in the world? And then do it.

> "...WHENEVER THINGS ARE OUT OF BALANCE, REMEMBER — WE CAN ALWAYS RETURN TO THE CROSSROADS AND BEGIN AGAIN."

Plans to keep advancing myself personally and professionally

Continue the fierce dedication to my path that is mine and only mine to walk. When required to make hard choices. marshaling support and resources along the way. Taking calculated risks. Bringing others along for the journey. Showing kindness.

Advice I would give to others

Two of my favorite quotes are:

- "Trust in Allah (God) and tie your camel," which is attributed to the prophet Muhammad (PBUH)

- "The arc of history is long but bends toward justice,"

which was paraphrased by Rev. Dr. Martin Luther King, Jr. from a sermon by Unitarian minister, Theodore Parker.

What I take away from these pithy words: There is a "beat" that runs under the universe that ultimately ensures everything "works out" even if it's beyond our own finite human understanding. And terrible things happen all the time — systemic forms of oppression and domination are real and must be dismantled. For all things, there is a balance between independence and interdependence. Being humble and being self-assured. Having a healthy and an unhealthy ego. There is no "arriving" at balance; it is a continual life-long dance. And whenever things are out of balance, remember — we can always return to the crossroads and begin again.

Notes & Reflections

> "YOU MUST PLACE INTEREST IN PRINCIPLE ABOVE INTEREST ON PRINCIPAL."
>
> - JULIAN BOND

Dr. Samuel Buxton

Joy and Pleasure in Small and Regular Wins

CHAPTER TWENTY-FOUR

Dr. Samuel Buxton

Human Health Toxicologist, Nickel Producers Environmental Research Association, Durham, NC

Dr. Buxton is a board-certified Toxicologist, with certifications in Europe and internationally, and proven experience in general toxicology, metal toxicology, genotoxicity, carcinogenesis, inhalation toxicology, and regulatory toxicology. He is knowledgeable in EU REACH, EU CLP, WHO and North American regulations. Dr. Buxton is an experienced project manager with years of experience managing multiple projects from conception to completion. He has also published in peer-reviewed journals.

Vision/Dream

I had a vision/dream as a young boy, around 10 years of age, of what I wanted to do with my life. That vision/dream has been a driving force for my de-

> "MY FAITH IN GOD GIVES ME PERSPECTIVE AND HOPE, AND MY RELATIONSHIP WITH PEOPLE, I HAVE FOUND, IS THE CURRENCY OF LIFE."

sire to always take the next step; I am not referring to a dream or vision one gets in sleep or a state of trance. I read a lot of books growing up. I spent my money to buy books, from novels to motivational books. I read a book every few days, 2-3 books a week. I still read a lot now, although it's mostly on Toxicology-related and general science materials.

Reading is one of the most important things that has contributed to my personal and professional growth. I have always been curious, and I found that this curiosity leads to learning. For example, although I didn't grow up with easy access to a computer, I knew that learning to type would be an invaluable skill for me one day. So as a young man in Ghana in the early 2000s, every opportunity I got, I went to internet cafés to learn to type using 'Mavis Beacon.'

It's important to also note that I have had a lot of challenging setbacks to my personal and professional growth. Almost no successful person will honestly tell you everything has been smooth sailing in their life. But the things that have helped me through all my challenges are my faith in God and my relationship with people. My faith in God gives me perspective and hope, and my relationship with people, I have found, is the currency of life.

I do not count myself as having attained ultimate success, lest I rest on my laurels and not strive to achieve more.

Regardless, I take joy and pleasure in the small and regular wins. For me, success is not measured in wealth but in my relationships, my contributions to society, and the meaningful difference I make in people's lives every day.

Success to me is growing every single day in knowledge and wisdom. I try to practice all of these every day to grow both personally and professionally.

Last but not least, my professional growth also includes attending conferences and meetings to exchange knowledge with others.

Notes & Reflections

" YOUR CHILDREN NEED YOUR PRESENCE MORE THAN YOUR PRESENTS. "

- REVEREND JESSE LOUIS JACKSON

25

Frances White Hall

No Shortcuts to Success

CHAPTER TWENTY-FIVE

Frances White Hall

Entrepreneur

Frances White Hall is an experienced Business Development Manager with a demonstrated history of working in the public safety industry. She is skilled in Nonprofit Organizations, Emergency Management, Team Building, Leadership, and Business Development. She is a strong consulting professional with a Bachelor of Arts (B.F.A.) in Design and Visual Communications, General, from University of Tennessee-Knoxville. She is currently on the entrepreneurial path.

No Shortcuts to Success

The key to all of my success was I was raised by two Christian parents who were committed to the upbringing and education of me and my four siblings. They married at 18 and 17 years old and remained married for 52 years until my father's death.

That upbringing guides all my character traits and guides my ethical core to this day.

Even when I err, I know how to seek forgiveness or in the professional setting, identify my mistakes and hold true to the lessons learned so that I do not repeat them.

Do not allow others to convince you that there are shortcuts to success. If it sounds too good to be true, it is. Trust that small voice within.

Finally, integrity lasts. Finish strong is my motto now that I am older. Finish strong!

> " ... INTEGRITY LASTS. FINISH STRONG IS MY MOTTO NOW THAT I AM OLDER. FINISH STRONG! "

Notes & Reflections

> "I'VE MISSED MORE THAN 9,000 SHOTS IN MY CAREER. I'VE LOST ALMOST 300 GAMES. TWENTY-SIX TIMES, I'VE BEEN TRUSTED TO TAKE THE GAME-WINNING SHOT AND MISSED. I'VE FAILED OVER AND OVER AND OVER AGAIN IN MY LIFE. AND THAT IS WHY I SUCCEED."
>
> **- MICHAEL JORDAN**

26

Dr. Aldrin Gomes

My Greatest Strength is My Optimism

CHAPTER TWENTY-SIX

Dr. Aldrin Gomes

Professor and Vice-Chair, Department of Neurobiology, Physiology, and Behavior, University of California, Davis

Dr. Gomes has published more than 200 papers in journals, books, and conference proceedings, including in top journals such as *Circulation and Science*. He is on the editorial board of seven journals and is a fellow of the American Heart Association (FAHA) and the cardiovascular section of the American Physiological Society (FCVS).

Qualities, Character Traits, Habits

My greatest strength is my optimism. I see a glass as half full instead of half empty. I don't let anything get me down for more than a few hours. However, I would not be able to achieve my

> "I AM HAPPIEST MAKING A DIFFERENCE IN PEOPLE'S LIVES, AND HAVING A TEENAGE DAUGHTER THAT STILL THINKS I AM COOL ADDS TO MY HAPPINESS."

goals without the joy I have doing what I do. Some people describe this as passion for what you do. This passion allows me to work harder than most. My drive takes over when things are taking longer than necessary to complete, and I take charge and make sure things get done.

Another important trait is that I learn from my mistakes. I consider mistakes as an opportunity to acquire new knowledge and improve.

Some habits I have that I think are important:
- I read 2-5 new non-fiction books every month.
- I have hobbies such as painting, photography, and dancing.
- I take care of myself. I eat healthy and exercise.
- I don't spend much time on social media.
- I pay attention to details.
- I am thankful for all that I have.
- I smile and laugh often.
- I enjoy helping people who want to be helped.
- I make time to talk to people I care about on a regular basis.

Advice
Planning your days/weeks/months and prioritizing your goals are very important. Achieving your goals often requires you to change your habits. If it does, make a commitment and change your habits.

What Success Means To Me
Being able to help others become successful and not worry about my own success. In short, success means happiness. I am happiest making a difference in people's lives,

and having a teenage daughter that still thinks I am cool adds to my happiness. However, I don't think of myself as successful; I think of myself as lucky to have what I have and to be as happy as I am.

Plans to keep advancing professionally and personally
I have a strong desire and commitment to learning. I plan to read even more books as well as learn advanced time management skills. However, I am also focused on working on goals that matter most to me. I plan on taking training courses that will help me better understand what causes student anxiety and stress while they are at University. With this knowledge I hope to implement new procedures to reduce the anxiety and stress that students experience.

My view is that since many students are having anxiety and stress, it is probably not the student, but the "system" we are currently using. Maybe it's time to change parts of the "system."

Personally, I am currently learning how to do pain relieving massages so I can hopefully help my mom reduce the pain she gets in her legs.

Notes & Reflections

> "I'M NOT COMFORTABLE BEING PREACHY, BUT MORE PEOPLE NEED TO START SPENDING AS MUCH TIME IN THE LIBRARY AS THEY DO ON THE BASKETBALL COURT."

- KAREEM ABDUL-JABBAR

27

Dr. Austin Coley

**The Kobe Bryant mentality,
"The best shot, is the next shot."**

CHAPTER TWENTY-SEVEN

Dr. Austin A. Coley

Neuroscientist / Adjunct Professor, University of California, San Diego

Dr. Coley is a Postdoctoral Fellow in Dr. Kay Tye's laboratory at The Salk Institute for Biological Studies and Adjunct Faculty in Cellular Neurobiology at The University of California, San Diego (UCSD). His work investigates the effect of neural circuits on behavior and state-dependent and region-specific cellular aberrations implicated in neuropsychiatric disorders.

Principles of Success

I often do not consider myself successful, and sometimes feel uncomfortable receiving praise for my accomplishments. The reason for this feeling is that I never allow myself to become complacent; I like to remain motivated to achieve a higher goal.

> "I NEVER ALLOW MYSELF TO GET DISCOURAGED AFTER A REJECTION, BUT IN FACT, I BECOME MORE MOTIVATED TO USE THIS AS AN OPPORTUNITY TO GET BETTER."

The lack of complacency keeps me humble. In my opinion, humility is the most underrated characteristic to sustain success over time, knowing that everyone has flaws and room for improvement. I also remind myself of the help I received along my journey.

My next principles of success are to become resilient and comfortable with failure. Failure is inevitable, but how you respond matters the most. I never allow myself to get discouraged after a rejection, but in fact, I become more motivated to use this as an opportunity to get better. I employ the Kobe Bryant mentality, "The best shot, is the next shot."

Lastly, I seek out constructive criticism to hone my skill set. I request help to improve my presentations, grant writing, and experimental designs. Therefore, I am not afraid of or discouraged by criticism. My favorite quote is "Man in the Arena" by Theodore Roosevelt, which describes an individual unafraid of critics, criticism, and the big moments. I practice this principle for my invited scientific seminar presentations.

Summary:
- Avoid complacency
- Remain humble
- Become resilient
- Be comfortable with failure
- Seek constructive criticism
- Be unafraid of the critic

Notes & Reflections

> **"LOTS OF PEOPLE WANT TO RIDE WITH YOU IN THE LIMO, BUT WHAT YOU WANT IS SOMEONE WHO WILL TAKE THE BUS WITH YOU WHEN THE LIMO BREAKS DOWN."**
>
> **- OPRAH WINFREY**

28

Brigadier General Clara L. Adams-Ender

Skills: Reading, Speaking, and Writing

CHAPTER TWENTY-EIGHT

Brigadier-General Clara L. Adams-Ender

Retired United States Army Officer

Brigadier-General Adams-Ender served as Chief of the United States Army Nurse Corps from September 1987 to August 1991. She was the first woman to receive her master's degree in military arts and sciences from the United States Army Command and General Staff College.

We All Need Mentors

I believe that no one succeeds in life without assistance from others. I had a mentor very early in my career and she guided me over the years. However, I have learned that my parents, who had 10 children, were probably my first mentors or, at least, they were wise teachers. They taught us all first, that we were somebody and to never associate with people who said we were not.

> "THREE SKILLS THAT I HAVE DEVELOPED THAT HAVE ASSISTED ME THROUGHOUT MY CAREER ARE READING (WHICH I LEARNED TO DO AT AGE 4), SPEAKING (WHICH I BEGAN TO DO AT AGE 6), AND WRITING, THE SKILL OF EXPRESSING ONESELF ON PAPER."

The second thing they taught us was that we could do and be anything we wanted to be, if we were willing to work hard and never give up. So when I started out in the world, I had self-esteem and I knew about persistence. I still practice those virtues till today. Other qualities that successful people develop are self-confidence, commitment, loyalty, and integrity.

There are some personal attributes which will enhance one's chances of achieving goals. Some of them are kindness, compassion, caring about others and being empathetic.

Three skills that I have developed that have assisted me throughout my career are reading (which I learned to do at age 4), speaking (which I began to do at age 6) and writing, the skill of expressing oneself on paper. These skills are lifelong, which means that they are valuable at every stage of one's life.

I have many plans to continue to advance myself both personally and professionally. I just released the seventh printing of my memoir. It is titled *My Rise to the Stars: How a Share-cropper's Daughter Became an Army General.*

During the Covid-19 pandemic (2020, 2021), I was involved in practicing my profession of nursing. I have been engaged in the practice for 61 years.

Notes & Reflections

> "LIFE IS A HARD BATTLE ANYWAY. IF WE LAUGH AND SING A LITTLE AS WE FIGHT THE GOOD FIGHT OF FREEDOM, IT MAKES IT ALL GO EASIER. I WILL NOT ALLOW MY LIFE'S LIGHT TO BE DETERMINED BY THE DARKNESS AROUND ME."

- SOJOURNER TRUTH

29

Dr. Solomon Mensah

Being the Best: Making it Impossible to be Ignored

CHAPTER TWENTY-NINE

Dr. Solomon Mensah

CEO, Therapeutic Innovations

Assistant Professor, Worcester Polytechnic Institute, Massachusetts

Dr. Solomon Mensah is the CEO and Co-Founder of Therapeutic Innovations and an Assistant Professor of Biomedical Engineering at Worcester Polytechnic Institute, Massachusetts, where he served as a Postdoctoral Fellow in 2020. He obtained his Ph.D. in Bioengineering in 2019 from Northeastern University and a Bachelor of Engineering (Biomedical Engineering) in 2014 from City University of New York.

Early Life: Living with Grandma

My parents were divorced before I was born; my mom was pregnant when they divorced. So, I grew up in a household where there was one parent at a time, but originally, my older brother and I

> "... I TECHNICALLY HAD TO WORK FULL TIME AND THEN ALSO GO TO SCHOOL. SO, I WAS WORKING 40 HOURS AND GOING TO SCHOOL 40 HOURS."

were sent to live with my grandmother at Takoradi (in the Western region of Ghana). So technically, in our childhood, my grandmother raised us; it was a single room. She had three kids of her own, including my mother, making it four. All of us were in the same single room. It was extremely challenging having to walk many miles to school. That was one thing that she was very particular about: making sure that, at least, we had a decent education.

Father's Support

When we grew up a bit, we moved from Takoradi to Accra (the capital of Ghana) to live with our father. In Accra, we lived in multiple areas, including Osu, Accra New Town, Kwabenya, Kasoa, and Dansoman. We didn't really have a stable location. We just kept moving from one place to the other. Through that, I completed my junior high school and got admission to Suhum Secondary Technical School. My father made sure that he did right by us, essentially, making sure that we got some kind of education.

Getting a Technical Education

From Suhum Sec Tech, I was not able to get admission to any of the universities. So, I ended up at Takoradi Polytechnic, which is now a technical university, where I studied Mechanical Engineering, Plant Option. After that, it took a while for me to get a job. I finally landed a temporary job at Guinness Ghana Brewers Limited, at Achimota. Now, through that, I worked my way up into becoming a permanent worker.

The U.S. Visa Lottery

From there, there was a friend of mine who I had attended

Takoradi Polytechnic with, who had then migrated to the States. He spoke about the American visa lottery program; he applied for that for me, and I got accepted into the program.

Coming to America

In the second year of working at Guinness, I left, and I was so eager to continue my education. Originally, I wanted to be a medical doctor, but due to the lack of resources, I ended up becoming a mechanical engineer, which is not a bad profession, but that wasn't my original idea.

When I migrated to America, I settled in New York City, the Bronx. And I quickly enrolled at City College of New York, which is part of the City University of New York network of universities. And this is at 145th and Amsterdam, somewhere around the border between Harlem and Manhattan.

Work and School: Only 80 Hours a Week!

I found out a program called biomedical engineering, which leveraged mechanical engineering principles to solve biological problems. I originally wanted to be a doctor; I didn't get the chance. I got the experience in mechanical engineering. And then all of a sudden, there's biomedical engineering where I can combine the two. I began to pursue that. It was difficult because I technically had to work full time and then also go to school. So, I was working 40 hours and going to school 40 hours. I was working at New Jersey Newark Beth Israel Hospital. I didn't have a car. So, you can imagine — you wake up in the morning, you go to school, and right after school, you hop on the New Jersey transit train, go to work, come back at almost 1:00 a.m., then you're up again the following morning, going to school. It was an extremely difficult time.

Introduction to the World of Research

During the process, I got introduced to research. I approached one of our senior faculty and I said I wanted to engage in research. And the purpose for that was to really understand what killed my grandmother; she had died of stroke. I did not understand why there was no treatment for that. I got interested in cardiovascular research and I joined the Wallace H. Coulter Cardiovascular Lab for Cardiovascular Dynamics and Biomolecular Transport at City College of New York. It was, and is still headed by Dr. John M. Tarbell. I began to pursue research, working full time, and then going to school full time. It was extremely challenging, but I was eager to understand more, because I was very intrigued by human physiology and I wanted to understand exactly how things worked.

I applied for the National Institutes of Health fellowship for undergraduate researchers, and I got accepted into it. So, I was getting support to pursue my research. I got paired with a postdoctoral fellow in the lab, Dr. Eno Ebong. And once her postdoctoral days were over, I also graduated. Then, she got a faculty position at Northeastern University. And then right

> "I ALWAYS KEPT IN MIND WHERE I CAME FROM AND WHAT I HAVE SURVIVED THROUGHOUT THE YEARS."

after that, she reached out and was wondering if I was interested in pursuing a PhD and I said, why not? So, I left New York, came to Boston, and while I was so used to working and doing multiple things at the same time, in the first year, it was so strange that all I was doing was just schoolwork and research.

A Passion for Medical Devices
I had a passion for medical devices because I took a trip to Africa once and I really wanted to understand what some of the challenges were in the healthcare system in terms of patient management. And I realized that we were struggling a lot with neonatal care. And so, I had that down as a top priority. When I came back to Boston, I said, you know what, I'm going to start a medical devices company. I did not know how to do that. But I began reading a lot and connecting with people that were in the entrepreneurial ecosystem in Boston.

The Birth of Therapeutic Innovations
I started a company, Therapeutic Innovations, with Anwar Upal, who is no longer working with us, and followed every incubation competition or pitch competition across Boston. We ended up as a finalist in the MassChallenge, which is one of the biggest entrepreneur innovation ecosystem competitions globally. And, through that, we got some visibility around Boston. We applied for an NSF (National Science Foundation) Corp grant, which we got. The funding was specifically for evidence-based customer discovery. And that means involving the customer in the design process, essentially making them co-designers in the process. We traveled extensively, myself and my team, across Africa, and Southeast Asia, just trying to engage

with the customer, and to understand what the specific needs were.

Completing the PhD

I was doing all that business-related stuff as well as pursuing my PhD. I got an NSF graduate fellowship award, which funded my PhD, and provided some kind of a stipend to help support my living. In my final year at Northeastern University, I was part of a committee that visited Worcester Polytechnic Institute for some kind of fact-finding endeavor. And, one of the senior faculty, after some interaction, thought I was going to be a good fit for the biomedical engineering program. So, even before I could graduate, I was offered a postdoctoral fellowship at WPI. I did that for a year, then through COVID, that was January of 2021, I got offered a full faculty position. So, I'm now beginning my research program at WPI.

Why the Single-minded Focus on Education?

Coming from where I came from, there weren't a lot of opportunities. And so, if you're given such an opportunity, you might as well take full advantage of it. It was very difficult trying to pursue so many things at the same time but I think the motivation was to be the best that I can in everything. I always kept in mind where I came from and what I have survived throughout the years. Also, knowing that this is an opportunity of a lifetime, you grab as much as you can. And whilst you're doing that, you pave the way for upcoming scientists and people of African descent to really understand that it's doable if you set your mind to it.

Dealing with Real or Perceived Barriers

At Northeastern University, you're the second Black person in the department. Even at WPI, in the faculty, we're just two people of African American descent. WPI's biomedical

> "MY PARENTS WERE ALWAYS THERE FOR ME, ALTHOUGH THEY WERE NOT TOGETHER. I COULD RELY ON THEM FOR WISDOM AND MOTIVATION."

engineering department has been awesome in creating a very welcoming environment for all sorts of people. But the point is: these things are there. That's just the social fabric of America. You can't deny that it's there because it shows up in subtle ways, and you see them, but I have made it a personal point to be the best at what I do in a way that I cannot be ignored — be the best at everything that I do so that you cannot ignore my influence in the field. If people have to put in X amount of effort, I decide to put in three X amount of effort, to just be extremely good at what I do. And you can just not ignore me in trying to look for people that are forces in the field that I'm in.

A Network of Supportive People
There have been a lot of people I could mention: people like Rida Lamptey Mills. She was a lady that I lived with when I came to America. She wanted me to go to school. So, she encouraged me a lot. My parents were always there for me, although they were not together. I could rely on them for wisdom and motivation. And then also, I found people within the Christian faith that were extremely supportive: my immediate pastor, Pastor Douglas Amagyei. The Lighthouse International Church were extremely supportive in helping me stay focused in this world of extreme challenges.

And of course, most importantly, my wife. It's difficult to not always be around and be busy traveling and working, but she understands. I think I've done a good job of selling the vision to her. And so, she has bought into the vision, and she understands the reason why I do the things I do. And I always keep her involved. I travel with her sometimes. So, she's engaged in what I'm doing and has a good understanding of what's going on. My siblings as well have all played a significant role in where I am.

Business and Academia: A Balancing Act

That's tough. I learned quickly during my undergrad, that, multitasking is one of the key driving forces to my success, that is, the ability to manage so many things at the same time and be good at all of them. One of the biggest things that I always tell the young and up-and-coming people is for them to learn to multitask. There are so many things that will be screaming for your attention. And then, in addition to that, if you spend so much time on things that are not profitable, you would end up with the status quo, working for people, and the person you're working for is probably sitting on a yacht somewhere, partying hard and drinking orange juice and you're busy working! So, the key is to multitask and, even if you work for people, you work for them only 8 hours out of the 24, the rest of the hours belongs to you. Whatever you do with those hours, it's your own responsibility, but I chose to pursue the normal route, where you go through academia. But then also, I decided to pursue my own thing. And so, what I do is to use up my academic wing as a research base for my startup company, where I give the students projects that are relevant to the startup company in a way to test the ideas. So, the students are able to build products that are functional, and then you route it through the startup company, and commercialize it that way.

Funding the Business

It's extremely challenging. My company is not a regular company; it's a social impact entrepreneurship innovation setup. Some of these investors want quick returns and triple returns on their investments. So, it's been very challenging getting funded. But just before the end of last year (2021), last summer, we got awarded a grant from the Paul Rogers Family Foundation that is propelling us into commercialization of our first product. See if you can think about starting a company around 2017, and four to five years later, getting your first break, it's extremely difficult. And that doesn't mean you are just relaxing. I was pursuing every opportunity that I could. But social impact entrepreneurship is not something that investors are very interested in or excited about because they want quick returns on their money.

In Seeking Supporters, Empathy is the Key

You have to tap into the empathetic aspect of people who will help support your project. And, I've made it a point not to deviate from that. I've met entrepreneurs, investors that encourage me to pursue profit first. But I am well driven by my past in the sense that I need to provide the necessary support for people that don't have the opportunities that we have; that's the driving force. I always keep that in my mind and set my eyes on that goal. It's taken a while, but we are here now.

Bringing People into the Business

First, you have to be empathetic. You have to have gone through something that would make you empathetic to the cause. I take you on the trips, into the dirt for you to look at the faces of these kids. And as you look at their faces and you look at their needs, that would stick with you. You look at the stories and how sometimes they have to let babies die because of lack of resources and it's going to hit you. So, my key thing is, you can teach the technical skills, but work ethic and empathy you can't teach. It's intrinsic and those are the things we look out for.

Paying Attention to Our Gifts

I was a kid that would always take the radio apart. I'm going to get punished by my dad but then when he buys me a new calculator,

> "...SUCCESS WOULD BE TO BE A GOOD HUSBAND AND A FATHER AND ENSURE THAT I GIVE MY KIDS ALL THE NECESSARY RESOURCES, NOT TO SPOON-FEED THEM OR BECOME A HELICOPTER DAD, BUT LET THEM HAVE THEIR OWN EXPERIENCE, BUT IN A GUIDED WAY."

I'll take it apart, because I wanted to find out what is in here that is making this thing behave the way it behaves. I was extremely curious. I think that is something that, even with my kids, you can see who is going to be the engineer and who's going to be a doctor. My older child is Ethan. He is very precise; he's a perfectionist. And he's a very gentle guy. He's very smart and very thoughtful. So, you already see the medical doctor in him. And then the little guy, Solomon, is all over the place, tearing things apart; he's breaking things, smashing things, throwing things, trying to yank things apart. He's all over the place and you can already see the engineer in him.

I think there are things we are just born with, and I think God gives us everything we need to be successful in this life before we come. The plan is to identify what those things are and pursue them. It is not to say that when they grow up and they want to become something else, I'm going to stop that. Whatever it is, would need to be explored. Sometimes, when I read biographies and I hear talks of people that have become successful, some of the traits that they talk about, are things that I already do unconsciously. It's almost like there are people that are brought to this life to succeed, by their temperament. There are people that are choleric, that is, they always want things done right on time, quickly, move fast. And then the phlegmatics, they take their time to think through stuff, very slow to act. And then there are the sanguines; they are always happy and excited about the least things, but they can't get the job done right and on time. It's as if we are all arranged in all of these temperaments. And then as you get to know your temperament, you get to know what the weaknesses of that temperament are. And then you work hard to either build those strengths or you get someone else to compensate for your weakness.

Definition of Success

In terms of my company, success will be, if I'm able to save one baby's life because you can't put value on a life. So, if through my device, I'm able to save one baby's life, that's all that matters to me.

In terms of my research, success would be when I'm able to engage in cardiovascular and cancer research and one of the things that I'm trying to do is to understand how to regenerate the vascular system in the course of a disease. So many diseases affect the vascular system; disease deteriorates the system. And that could lead downstream to organ failure and some other things. So, what I'm trying to do is to develop procedures and strategies to reinforce the vascular system against the adverse effects of diseases such as cancer, hypertension, sepsis and others, so that the vascular system can be strong to fight against those kinds of diseases. So, success for me in my research is if I'm able to come up with a regeneration strategy to prevent vascular deterioration from these diseases.

In terms of life, success would be to be a good husband and a father and ensure that I give my kids all the necessary resources, not to spoon-feed them or become a helicopter dad, but let them have their own experience, but in a guided way.

Notes & Reflections

" IT'S SO MUCH FUN TO WATCH GOOD PEOPLE GET GOOD THINGS IN LIFE. "

- TREVOR NOAH

30

Dr. Darius B. Dawson

Focus on Social Responsibilities and Services

CHAPTER THIRTY

Dr. Darius B. Dawson

Medical School Instructor/Investigator, Baylor College of Medicine, Houston, Texas

Dr. Dawson is a Core Investigator with the South Central Mental Illness Research, Education, and Clinical Center and the Houston Center of Innovation for Quality, Effectiveness, and Safety at the Michael E. DeBakey Veterans Affairs Medical Center and Instructor in the Department of Medicine at Baylor College of Medicine in Houston, Texas. His work focuses on tobacco cessation treatment for African American veterans.

Definition of Success for Me

My first goal in becoming a successful individual was to define what success meant for me. For some, success equates to a salary number, a list of accolades, or a job title. For me, success equates to the amount of time spent each day focused on social

> "... PEOPLE REMEMBER THOSE THAT MADE THEM FEEL SAFE, POSITIVE, AND ACCOMPLISHED."

responsibilities and services that I am passionate about. I have found that following my passion has led to development of expertise in a specific area, which in turn has led to advancement in my career. However, for me, advancement in career would not be enough to feel successful. I feel successful because I go to work each day and have the privilege to be passionate about what I do.

I also pride myself on being approachable, compassionate, and kind. Anyone can be a great employee, the most accomplished in their field, or attain the highest level of power. However, not everyone is easy to work with, someone that people want to be mentored by, or an asset to a team or working system.

The best advice I received at the early stages of my graduate training was that people remember those that made them feel safe, positive, and accomplished. Just as I continue to work on gaining levels of expertise, I am always pushing myself to be the person I want others to be in times of crisis, confusion, or despair.

One of the biggest hurdles I faced was racial/ethnic prejudice, due to being a Black man. The higher I have climbed in education and in my career, the more prejudice I have faced (i.e., microaggressions, exclusivity, internalized racism). However, I have learned that a positive and accurate perception of myself is the most important and the best defense against prejudice. I define who I am and what I stand for, not other people. I had to learn to acknowledge my own capabilities and create my own pathway towards my goals. Eventually, I ended up at an organization that welcomed my background and experiences, while championing who I was and what I could contribute. I have learned that allies and supporters come in all races, genders, and backgrounds; you must be patient enough for them to find you.

"It takes a village" is a very true statement when it comes to the success of an individual. All of my success and accomplishments are built on the backs of many others and due to the continued support of many others.

I had two supportive parents that provided me with resources and psychological safety to explore what career I wanted to pursue. I was afforded the privilege of trial-and-error from an early age while deciding my interests. As I became an adult, I had key mentors that were influential in my development. These mentors not only invested time and effort, but they also used their own professional connections to help further my advancement.

When the opportunity has presented itself, I have done my best to show up. However, some opportunities require the support and facilitation of others who believe in your future success.

Any individual can have resilience and determination. However, if individuals are met with resistance or prejudice, their success will be limited.

Notes & Reflections

> "I'M NO LONGER ACCEPTING THE THINGS I CANNOT CHANGE...
> I'M CHANGING THE THINGS I CANNOT ACCEPT."
>
> - DR. ANGELA Y. DAVIS

31

Kirk McDonald

Don't use someone else's ruler to measure your success.

CHAPTER THIRTY-ONE

Kirk McDonald

CEO, GroupM North America

Kirk McDonald leads 6,500 people at the forefront of changes in the technology, media, and marketing arenas. He is a member of GroupM's Global Leadership Team, and is a major player in crafting the organization's strategies and working with agency leadership to deliver top-of-the-line solutions for clients. Prior to GroupM, Kirk served as Chief Business Officer at Warner Media's Xandr where he was in charge of sales, communications, product marketing, marketing strategy, and execution.

My Mother's Gift: A Powerful Quote

Create and understand the principles of your work ethic. My mother offered me the following quote for my High School yearbook, and it has been the summation of my work ethic and drive throughout my professional career.

> "FEED YOUR CURIOSITY. YOUR CURIOSITY IS A POWERFUL NAVIGATIONAL TOOL IN CAREER DEVELOPMENT AND GROWTH."

"The heights by great men reached and kept were not attained by sudden flight, but they while their companions slept, were toiling upward in the night."

- Henry Wadsworth Longfellow

This life lesson is a reminder that smart hard work, and perseverance will create the advantages you need to exceed and get to your fullest potential. For this reason, I don't aspire to be, or worry about being, smarter than anyone else in the room. Instead, I celebrate the wisdom that comes from the collaboration of teamwork. My confidence comes from knowing that I will usually work harder than others to achieve my best.

Don't use someone else's ruler to measure your success. Professional success starts with personal success, and personal success is just that, it's personal. You must be honest with yourself about what drives you and what rewards you. The achievements will never feel good, until you create the context for them.

Personally, I measure success in the outcomes of work, not the authorship or even the ownership. That's what works for me and allows me to create the professional space for partnerships and collaboration. When we hold things too close, we often starve our ideas of the food/fuel that good ideas need to flourish. The key is to have an honest acceptance of your measures of success, and then only keep your score to yourself.

Feed your curiosity. Your curiosity is a powerful navigational tool in career development and growth. Ultimately, you can find success anywhere and, in any field, as long as you measure success on your own terms. Therefore, following your curiosity rewards you immensely. Your ideation and innovation will be found/developed at the leading edge of your curious professional explorations.

Becoming an expert in your craft requires a passionate curiosity for your area of learning and development. Curiosity has led me into every new area of professional learning and career development. I'm grateful for it, and continue to find ways to feed it every day.

Notes & Reflections

> "I CERTAINLY WASN'T SEEKING ANY DEGREE, THE WAY A COLLEGE CONFERS A STATUS SYMBOL UPON ITS STUDENTS. MY HOMEMADE EDUCATION GAVE ME, WITH EVERY ADDITIONAL BOOK THAT I READ, A LITTLE BIT MORE SENSITIVITY TO THE DEAFNESS, DUMBNESS AND BLINDNESS THAT WAS AFFLICTING THE BLACK RACE IN AMERICA. NOT LONG AGO, AN ENGLISH WRITER TELEPHONED ME, ASKING QUESTIONS. ONE WAS, "WHAT'S YOUR ALMA MATER?" I TOLD HIM, "BOOKS.""

- MALCOLM X

32

Dr. Christopher Boone

**An Insatiable Hunger
for Knowledge & Information**

CHAPTER THIRTY-TWO

Dr. Christopher Boone

Vice President, Global Head, Health Economics & Outcomes Research (HEOR), AbbVie; Professor, Wagner School, New York University

Christopher P. Boone, Ph.D., has made his mark as a strategist, global executive, social scientist, and data technologist who champions the power of real-world evidence, health informatics, and enterprise data and analytics to transform global health. Chris has been honored as a Global Top 100 Innovator in Data and Analytics (2019, 2020) among many other awards.

Family Background

I grew up in pretty much a single-parent home. My mother was married a few different times. They weren't to my father, and they weren't very long marriages. That's why I say single-parent home, in a relatively

> "IT'S ALMOST LIKE THE MORE YOU LEARN, THE MORE YOU REALIZE YOU DON'T KNOW ANYTHING. THE IRONY IS WHEN YOU'RE YOUNGER, YOU THINK YOU KNOW EVERYTHING, AND YOU TRULY KNOW NOTHING."

impoverished area in Dallas, Texas. I attended Dallas Public Schools before making my way to the University of Tulsa. I was a student-athlete in the earlier stages in my life, which I think provided a gateway in many respects. It served as a great opportunity to focus on a life beyond what was found in my immediate surroundings. It forced you to focus on academics and athletics and not just be caught up in the many things that are happening in the environment.

Key Moments of Decision in Early Life

One of the pivotal academic decisions in my childhood was made by my mother. I was a first-generation college graduate and not just in my immediate family, but my extended family as well. Sadly, my brother and my sister did not graduate high school, so I was the only one of the three kids to graduate from high school and then college. So, you can see these three kids; you got this one who's very focused on achieving, but my mother made a very pivotal decision. I was in eighth grade, and it came down to making a determination about where I was going to go to high school. And I had this option to go to a premier magnet high school in the city. I really wanted to go to the local high school because they had better sports — where your friends were and you thought maybe, it's just where you wanted to be because it was familiar, but she was adamant. It was rare that she was very adamant about things, but for some reason, for that decision, she was very adamant about it: "No, you're going to this magnet school."

Now this magnet school was like 18 miles from my house. It was on the other side of the city. So, I literally bused across the city every day for four years, but it ended up being the most meaningful decision in my young adolescent years, because then, I was surrounded by other kids who shared similar life goals and visions to go to college and to do great things in life, which was positive reinforcement to the rest of my journey. So, it was a very pivotal decision for me very early on.

Education – Going All the Way to PhD
In terms of how much education has become a part of my life, I would say to some degree, it was a bit serendipitous. It was always organic. No one in my family had a bachelor's degree. Some didn't even have high school diplomas. So, to get out to high school, it felt like it was a big deal, but then, when I went and got my bachelor's degree, it was like, "Oh my gosh, he's really a big deal." So, they didn't even know what a master's or a PhD was! I remember my grandmother saying, "Wait, you're in school again. Why are you in school again? I thought you already did that." And I said, "I'm getting my master's degree."

I recognized early on, when I started my career, I had this vision that I really wanted to be a CEO of a public health system in the U.S., and I felt it would be my way of impacting communities that were underserved and marginalized when it came to their healthcare needs, and I knew in order for me to do that, I needed to have a master's degree. So that was the first impetus. Now, the PhD, I don't know what I was thinking then. I knew at some point when I started to get into administration that I liked the idea of potentially teaching in the latter part of my career, maybe, a post-retirement move.

So, I thought maybe I would do it later in life. When I really got into the master's degree or graduate level studies, I became like a sponge for information. The bachelor's degree was just very formative; it felt like it was foundational, but when I got into graduate school, and it was very focused and there were things that I saw that were directly applicable to what I cared about, I became a sponge for information. The PhD became somewhat inevitable because I wanted to dive deeper in my understanding of how things worked. I felt like there was more of a gravitational pull to it.

And honestly, I did my master's and my PhD while working, full time, which seems crazy when I look back. I don't know how I did it, but it did require me to go through education the entirety of the year. There was no break. I attended courses in the fall, the spring, and the summer semesters in order to stay on track with those who were pursuing their degrees full time, which is a rather significant commitment, considering you're taking care of children, working in a very demanding job, and all the other extracurricular activities. I think when you're very committed and you're passionate about something, as with anyone and any occupation, you don't think about it when you're doing it. It's just the passion that fuels you and you push through it.

Having Multiple Harvard Certificates
I'm thinking about doing another, but when I did the certificates it was almost like a personal insecurity that I didn't know enough. It's almost like the more you learn, the more you realize you don't know anything. The irony is when you're younger, you think you know everything, and you truly know nothing. When I pursued the Harvard Kennedy School certifications, I needed to know more. I needed to go deeper. I needed to understand more. I needed to absorb more, and as a byproduct of doing those programs, it was quite fascinating in that, in one of those programs that I was in, you had the former president of Finland in the course. The exposure that you get to the great minds and leaders

in our world interested in the same topics was fascinating. Granted, she wasn't the sitting president anymore, but she was sitting in the Harvard Kennedy school class with me seeking that deeper understanding of healthcare policy. For me, I think I've always had this insatiable hunger for knowledge and information. I was just spurred by the fact that I didn't know enough. I don't know if that's rooted in some feeling of inadequacy, but I think it's just, "I don't know enough. I need to know more if I want to do more. If I want to do better, if I want to make an impact, I need to know more," and so, that's what fuels me.

I read a lot, but I'm very focused in the things that I read: a lot of leadership books, a lot of books around health policy, and healthcare data. All the things that you see me speaking and talking about are the things that I tend to immerse myself in because I'm very passionate about those particular topics, and that's the way I think I can make a positive impact on the world.

The Corporate Sector: The Black Experience
It's been tough, and I think for me, I've taken such an illogical, nonlinear approach to my career. I'm a senior leader in one of the world's largest pharmaceutical companies, but I didn't start my career in pharmaceuticals. Many of my peers have spent their entire professional lives in pharma. Then you have a guy who literally started working at a pharma company in 2017 and has ascended to new heights (speaking in 2022). So, I think it seems illogical to most people that a guy who has spent the vast majority of his career (prior to biopharma) in healthcare systems, nonprofit organizations, and a boutique consulting firm, could rise to become a senior leader in a global pharmaceutical company.

Learn to Adapt; Find Your Swim Lane

I think one of the key pieces of advice I always share with my mentees is around being open and being adaptive. The key is to allow yourself to pivot without fear when the time is right.

You are always going to have your fair share of obstacles or challenges in life. Quite frankly, I still experience many life challenges. I tend to believe the challenges become greater the higher you rise because there's a bigger target on your back. Even though it may seem to folks that you have this African-American leader who's risen up the ranks, they do not always seem to understand and appreciate the added pressure: the bigger target, and all these things that come along with that. With the added position and "power" comes this added responsibility and added burden that I didn't necessarily feel when I was in an earlier phase in my career. Granted, I faced challenges there, but I was always willing, which I find some of my peers and others not willing to do, that is, to make the necessary changes to put myself in this position. That requires a certain level of self-confidence.

> "...I'VE ALWAYS FOUND SWIM LANES WHERE I'M ABLE TO PROGRESS. AND I ADAPT AND I CONSTANTLY KEEP CHANGING AND KEEP MOVING UP RATHER THAN TRYING TO FORCE MYSELF THROUGH SITUATIONS THAT, FRANKLY, ARE JUST A BRICK WALL..."

Recipient of 40 Under 40 Leaders in Health Award (2017); Presented by the National Minority Quality Forum

You got to believe in yourself, but it also requires a sense of self-awareness, like knowing what environments you thrive the best in. I think oftentimes as African Americans, we try to force fit ourselves into situations. We try to be that square peg, without recognizing that sometimes the environment is not conducive for your success, and therefore, you can think you're going to change the environment, or you can either change yourself or change the situation and allow yourself to thrive. I've always been one to do the latter. I've always accepted environments for what they were. We can talk about corporate America, and say it's race, and I will tell you, I agree, but I've always found swim lanes where I'm able to progress. And I adapt and I constantly keep changing and keep moving up rather than trying to force myself through situations that, frankly, are just a brick wall; you're not going to be able to break through it. That's what works for me.

How to Stand Out

I didn't want to believe at first that I brought superior communication, superior knowledge or superior leadership to the workplace because it seems like there's some sort of arrogance, and I think coming from humble beginnings, culturally, African Americans, generally, we're taught to be very humble about skills or talents that you have. And so, it's rare to find people who just say, "Hey! look at me, I have some superiority." You're just not raised that way. One of the greater challenges for Black folks in the U.S. is because of that cultural element and being taught that you're not supposed to do that. Now, Kanye West is an exception. His mother raised him on the other end of the spectrum: "You're everything, and you can change the world," which I think is great for him because he believes it, but I wasn't raised that way. I had to overcome the conditions of how I was raised in order to be more confident to allow myself to thrive. I had to reprogram myself in some respects to say, "No, you are good," and "It's okay for you to feel confident that you have superior leadership, superior knowledge, or superior communication skills," and then, once you're able to overcome that, you take that confidence into your work environment. Granted, you still have to maintain, if nothing else, the perception that you're humble; you have to be grounded in some sort of humility, but still exhibit those superior talents and skills. And yes, I think that because of those things (superior communication, superior knowledge, and superior leadership), it has given many senior leaders more confidence in my ability to execute and to deliver on things and to lead teams.

Information Technology
I was a management information systems major in undergrad, so I started off on the I.T. side, building systems and implementing them into hospitals. And at that time, I thought I wanted to get out of that because I didn't want to be an I.T. guy. I thought that was very limiting. Remember, I wanted to be CEO of a health system and it's rare to find an I.T. guy that was going to be leading the health system. You will be working for the CEO, but you wouldn't be the person. I tried to divorce myself from that sort of natural skill that I had because it came really easy to me. I found success doing it.

When I ultimately ended up at the American Heart Association earlier in my career, that's when I really got into the hardcore data for analysis or the analytics side of it to support clinical care and decision-making, and I honestly took that role because I was in the midst of my PhD. They said, "Hey, we have this one-year fellowship role," and I thought, "That's perfect. That'll give me a year to finish this, and I can finish my dissertation, and then I can go off and do something else."

But I got into the role and a month into the job, they say, "Hey, you know, we really want you to be one of our directors leading this for us again," because they saw communication, they saw leadership, they saw knowledge. And I thought, "Okay, sure, why not?" So, I did that. But I'll tell you an interesting story about that. I was doing it and a year into that job, my immediate manager, who was the vice president of this function, was being reassigned to another job. She was on the fast track, and so they reassigned her to another role in the American Heart Association, which means her role became vacant. Now everyone thought, "Oh, this guy, he's an obvious choice. I mean, he's a young guy, he knows this stuff. He's a great leader. He's a great communicator, whatever." They did not give me that role. They said, and this is when I felt the blackness, the racism, they tried to say: "Well, it's because he hadn't spent as much time with the AHA." They got all these random excuses; they went and hired someone from the outside who had zero experience at the American Heart Association who just happens to be a white man, and they were expecting me to report to this guy. That preempted me leaving the American Heart Association and going to Avalere Healthcare, which is a boutique firm in DC, which actually ended up being a great move because it set everything else up.

So, everything happened the way it was supposed to happen, but there have been different moments in my career where that has happened consistently. I was willing to make the change because I could have just said, I'm just going to stay at the American Heart Association, and I'll figure it out, I'd work for this new guy, even though I know I should have been in the job, and I'd just wait it out, but I didn't. I said, "You know what? I know my worth. I know what I bring to the table." They made their decision; now, I'll make mine. So, I left.

> "WHEN YOU START SAYING I'M SUCCESSFUL, THAT TO ME FEELS LIKE COMPLETION. IT'S LIKE SAYING YOU'RE AT THE END, I'VE COMPLETED MY JOURNEY, AND I DON'T FEEL LIKE THAT. I FEEL IN MANY WAYS THAT I'M JUST GETTING STARTED, TO BE HONEST."

Balancing Corporate Leadership with Being a Professor

I prioritize teaching. I think teaching for me is fulfilling. It doesn't pay much, but it pays dividends in the fact of me connecting with students — being able to mentor and coach. NYU (New York University) does a tremendous job of creating such a diverse student population that comes from all walks of life, and I really love that. I love that university, and everything that it stands for because it's very progressive in the US when it comes to reaching all people. So, I make it a priority. It's tough because I'm a senior leader in this big corporation, and then, I'm up here at night, teaching the course. Right now, I mean, all my courses are through Zoom. We have weekly lectures and assignments and I'm grading all their assignments too. So, it's a pretty big commitment, but I think it's something that I'm so passionate about that I don't think about it as much.

Serving on Corporate Boards

I'm on the board of directors for a company called Global Medical Response, a private for-profit company that is going public in the next 1-2 years. They were public and they went private and are going public again; it's a $5 billion company. I'm the only person of color on this entire board, but I've learned to not bring race to the forefront of my mind. I just say, "Hey, I'm here for a reason to just perform, just do what I do," and I've learned to do that and it's helped me, but I think serving on a board, you have similar experiences to what you find in senior level jobs in these big companies: you're still with the same cast of characters. So, we, as a people, can experience some of the same things. I think it's slightly different though because when you're on the board, you're technically in a different position than just being an employee for the company, which introduces a new dynamic when engaging with others.

Definition of Success

Success for me is a person who achieves their own self-defined goals, whatever they are personally, professionally or otherwise, and you reach it to where it's to the point of your satisfaction. If you can look back and say I've accomplished all that I set out to accomplish. And for some, that'll be higher in personal life, some may be higher in professional life. It's really difficult. I think that, for me, I haven't achieved that point yet. I think I've achieved a tremendous amount of success if I listen to others because either I've beaten the odds or I've achieved more personal and professional success than they have, but I haven't achieved all that I feel I could have achieved. So, therefore I wouldn't call myself successful yet. When you start saying I'm successful, that to me feels like completion. It's like saying you're at the end, I've completed my journey, and I don't feel like that. I feel in many ways that I'm just getting started, to be honest.

A Passion for Reading

I'm one of those folks who will read most things at a high level, but I won't go deep with it; it's just like a sort of genuine curiosity, like, just read this and see what this is about, but I go deep and I read things that are significant and important to me. And that's leadership, for example. One of the folks who started me on that journey was at one of my first internships. I had a preceptor who was a woman, a White woman, and she sat me down and said, "I've noticed something about you; you seem to have some quality about you with leadership. I want you to read this for me and I want you to write a report about it." She started giving me these articles. Then she started assigning me books.

And then, every week I had to read something and write about it and then talk to her about it. And it would just happen that the topic was about leadership and different leaders and their different philosophies and approaches to various problems. And one of those leaders she had me read about was Colin Powell. I became obsessed with Powell; I thought he was the most poised, thoughtful, selfless sort of leader. He spoke less, but when he spoke, it meant something, and just the class and dignity, integrity that this man had, I admired it so much, and he was the guy that I wanted to emulate.

And what this woman put me on is a journey of seeking deeper understanding and recognizing talents that I may naturally have, and that I have to continuously nurture and grow and expose. And so, I started to just do that with everything, with things that I felt were my natural talents, gifts or interests. I would just go deeper. That's what set up all the degrees and certifications and everything that I've done. I just became a lifelong student of these various topics, and one thing that I wish I could do more of is write. I write for myself (in a journal). I just wish I published it more.

For me, writing is therapeutic: it's about experiences and situations, and I start telling myself, "I really have to start making these things available more to others."

Advice to Young People

What advice would I give to young people? It really depends on what aspects one is talking about. I would tell people to live a full life, to be authentically themselves, to recognize that you're not for everyone. So, if you're going to be authentically you, and also on the other side of it, not everybody is going to like you for being you. But there's some element of being able to be true to yourself that I think folks have to respect. I think one of the things that I learned over the years is always asking myself when I get all these invitations to do these speaking events or these guest lectures. For example, I'm flying up to MIT in Cambridge to do a guest lecture tomorrow night, and it's one of the things that I do and say so casually now. I started asking folks: "Why do people keep inviting me to do this stuff?" In one case, the person's like, "No!" And I said, "No, I really don't know. I really don't know." And he goes, "Well, what I appreciate about you is that you're so relatable, and you're so authentic in what you say and what you've written." So, that's the "it" factor for me.

Be Authentic

The thing that I've learned, and I had this executive coach last year tell me, you really got to lean more into your authenticity, something about being an authentic leader. And I kept hearing it from all these different people, so I thought, I got to really sort of lean into this. So, I think, my advice to people, I wish I would've just known that earlier on because I think we're taught that you have to be perceived as someone else, as some prototype, if you will. And that prototype just doesn't look like us, and I've learned to sort of lean into all that makes me now, and what that means.

What I will tell a young person too is that it doesn't mean that you go off and act like a buffoon, and just tell people this is authentically you and you got to accept it.

That is not what it means. I also think young folks have got to spend more time with themselves to know themselves. They're living the expectations and perceptions of their friends, family, anybody around them, in their immediate circle that they don't even know themselves. And I think that's somewhat normal because if people are constantly telling you, you're this way as a child, guess what, you start to believe it. When Kanye West was growing up, his mother told him "You're the greatest thing ever, and he still believes it." He may very well be.

We are what we consume, what we hear, what we believe about ourselves. I don't know if we spend enough time learning who we are for ourselves and embracing whatever that inner self is. And I think that the fact that I was able, despite circumstances, to raise who my inner self was and say, "I'm going to stand firm in what I believe. Even though it may not be what the majority thinks or feels, it's what I feel, and it's what I believe, and it's what I think of myself. And I'm just going to walk with that." And sometimes knowing that, it may be a lonely road that you walk. Sometimes, there may be people there, but whether there are people there or not, it doesn't matter.

The most important point is getting to be true to yourself. I was sharing a story with a mentor about getting this praise from some guy – a random guy who was praising me. I was sharing it with him because I felt so good about it, and he looked at me. This is a Black guy; he's a mentor. He looks at me and goes, "Hmm, why do you seem so impressed by this guy telling you this?" And I respond, "Well, he just told me that I'm great." He said, "You're listening," and I told him, "I'm not getting the sense that you are as excited about this as I am." And he says, "Well, what if the guy had told you, you did a horrible job, and you were not very good, how would you react?" I couldn't help but wonder why he was asking me hypotheticals when that was not what had happened.

The lesson he was teaching me is to never allow the perception of others to shape what you feel about yourself, whether positive or negative. That was one of the greatest pieces of advice he could have shared with me. Throughout my career, I've seen people who praise me, and I've seen those same people literally criticize me the very next day. So, they would put me on an emotional rollercoaster. So, that pearl of wisdom that he shared with me was just priceless because now when people praise me, I just humbly say, thank you.

And when they ridicule me, I'll say, thank you. So, I think one of the things that I would share with young people is 'Know thyself, trust thyself, believe thyself, and don't let others influence thyself."

Plan for Further Self-Improvement
I think the way that I want to improve myself is being present in the moment. As someone who's always sought to achieve the next thing, it's always been challenging to live in the moment and savor the moment. I think I've sometimes automatically jumped to the next thing, and I jump to the next thing and I jump to the next thing. And I'm always chasing something that I probably will never reach because it's always running, but I rarely look back and say, "Wow, I did all of that." And I think the downside of constantly chasing is life will quickly pass you by be-

cause we're not getting any younger. I'm getting older, and I keep chasing something and I don't take the time to appreciate the things that I was able to do or the life I have built in that moment. I know one should never say, "I've done it all. I should stop." But I do think there are moments in life when we should smell the roses: "I've done good work, I've achieved some great things, and it's okay to celebrate yourself." That would be number one — being present in the moment.

The other thing that I would say as far as being present is *being present with the people that you care about most*. I think when you're chasing dreams and you're doing these things, it's easy to leave people behind or forget about folks and be on this journey by yourself, which to some degree you have to do, but at the end of the day, when you're on your deathbed, who will be there with you, and knowing who those folks are, the folks who you should grace with that time, the same way they've graced you and blessed you with their time and their support. Those are things that I seek to improve, being present, and celebration of success and celebration of life with my loved ones.

Notes & Reflections

> "THE DAY THE SOLDIERS STOP BRINGING YOU THEIR PROBLEMS IS THE DAY YOU STOPPED LEADING THEM. THEY HAVE EITHER LOST CONFIDENCE THAT YOU CAN HELP THEM OR CONCLUDED THAT YOU DO NOT CARE. EITHER CASE IS A FAILURE OF LEADERSHIP."

- GENERAL COLIN POWELL

33

Dr. Joseph A. Bailey II

"Me/We"

CHAPTER THIRTY-THREE

Joseph A. Bailey II, MD, FACS

Founding Owner, JAB Lifeskills Foundation; Orthopaedic Surgeon

Dr. Joseph A. Bailey II was born in Pine Bluff, Arkansas, and reared in Wilson and Greensboro, North Carolina where he became an Eagle Scout (twice, necessitated by racism). Then he attended the University of Michigan, Morehouse College, and Meharry Medical School; interned at Los Angeles County General Hospital; and as a USA Air Force captain in the Philippines, was chief of the Family Practice Clinic in charge of 10,000 troops and their families.

"ME/WE"

> "SUCCESS IN AFRICAN TRADITION IS NOT ABOUT ACHIEVING MATERIAL THINGS, BUT RATHER MAKING DEDICATED EFFORTS TO DISPLAY A GIVEN HUMAN'S ASSIGNED DIVINE PLAN FOR SPIRITUALLY UPLIFTING THE "ME/WE"."
>
> - JAB II

The four groups of Black People to whom I give the most of my Legacy Destination attention are the children; those youth who want to be "Somebody" and do not know how to go about it; the Poor who struggle through no fault of their own; and Ambitious Isolated Individualists (of which I am one).

Over the years, I have discovered that Enslaved minded people only want what they want to get: benefits for the moment — and not what they need for "ME/WE" long-term Well-Being Improvement. Thus, since my gift-giving — starting in the mid-1970s — has not carried the degree of benefit I desire, my first expansion involved trying to achieve this by various means. One was to write books on what I had been researching of the Black Mind, dating back to 200,000 BC. From 2003 to the present, I have written 80 on Black History, including 47 Dictionaries on Ancient African and Afrocentric terms. I thought I could get "After School" programs taught by Black teachers to include the use of my books — but that did not work out well. But actually, I do not know because I occasionally hear about their benefit from people around the USA. An example is a Psychologist in Michigan who gave a Black Family one of my articles I had written 16 years prior. Certain of my Mentees mention things I told them far back in time.

JAB II
ISOLATED INDIVIDUALIST'S EVOLUTION: On the edge of the campus of Pine Bluff A & M — or Arkansas State College — now the University of Arkansas at

Pine Bluff — I was born on the second floor of a grocery store. There, my Dad was head of the Department of Social Sciences and Dean of History (see Joseph A. Bailey Sr., *From Africa to Black Power* and Bailey II, *Word Stories Surrounding African American Slavery*).

At age 3, my sister Joselyn would take me for a walk and I would invariably sit down in the street or the sidewalk or on the lawn and "Mull"— what I now consider "Just Being" (i.e., bathing in the inner world of the Cosmic Organism). Then Dad, Mother, my sister and I drove a Ford to California. Along the way I was impressed with the colorful artifacts of Amerindians. My parents bought a blanket for me to which I was extremely attached, whether for cover while sleeping or as a companion during waking hours. I also saw an overturned car and could not understand why my parents did not turn it over and bring it along.

In Los Angeles — which I thought to be the greatest place on earth — I slept on Uncle Cecil's back porch. The wonderful fragrance of orange trees awakened me each morning to a 75 degree temperature. Although this was in the city, no houses were in sight. After a few weeks there, we drove the scenic route to Minnesota, driving through the great Sequoia Forest where trees were so big as for a highway to be built through some. That made such a lasting impression that to this day I would like to make the trip again in an RV camper. We arrived in Minnesota to live in an all-White community.

MINNESOTA: As a 3-year-old, during the middle of the Great Depression, I enjoyed the snow — that would get as high up as to reach the second floor windows at times. Temperatures would drop to 40 below zero. Yet, I had to take a bath in cold water every morning and that took so much Courage as to leave me with a lasting impression concerning me entering cold water. For example, I went to Catalina, stuck my toe in the ocean water, and it took 30 minutes to drum up the courage to jump in.

For the last third of my life, my shower has been on the second floor, thus taking a while for the water to heat up. Since I do not want to waste water, I turn it on a trickle so as to lather my body — all in cold water — before turning it on full blast for a few seconds so as to wash off the soap. We could only afford to heat the kitchen and so Mother would wrap heated bricks to put under the covers at the foot of my bed. This meant running as fast as possible up the stairs and all the way around to the back of the hall — jumping in bed and rubbing my feet on the sheets as fast as possible. Since there was very little money, we lived by fishing — each family being allowed to catch 60 fish — but we could eat all we wanted at any of the 10,000 lakes. One time, I did something to cause all the fish to be lost and thus we started over, getting our quota in an hour. At age 4, my parents divorced and I remember swinging on my Dad's arm begging him not to go. At this point, I decided that the reason for the divorce was that we did not have enough money and thus self-declared I would become financially successful so as to bring my family back together again — something like being a physician.

My Mother was a genius in sacrifice, working 16 hours a day — often outside, even during the winter for 50 cents a day. Still, she found time to take us to free Art Museums and Music festivals — always reading the brochures, such as "Blue Boy," to us as we paused at each painting. The orchestral music helped me form concepts of Gentleness — as by taking the hard edges off what had to be done in order to remain in a quiet mindset while moving harmoniously in the flow. She would also read to us at bed-

> **PAY WHATEVER IT TAKES TO OBTAIN A SUPERIOR EDUCATION (I.E., DEVELOPING YOUR TALENTS AND SKILLS) RELATED TO YOUR CAREER, FOR THIS BREAKS THE VICIOUS CYCLE OF POVERTY AND IS THE WAY TO RISE ABOVE POVERTY.**

time and that really stimulated my imagination. I spent a tremendous amount of time lying on my back and making cartoons out of the clouds. Mother, in order to work for a Jewish family, would lock me in my room upstairs, and turn the radio on to an Italian Opera station; from this, I learned the valuable lesson of how to entertain myself and enjoy being with myself. I knew opera so well that I practiced singing it backwards. Much of the rest of the time I would hear my sister play Classical Music all day — and she even gave a concert at age 7.

We had dental work and health care done at the University of Minnesota where my Dad was attending. At that time we were Christian Science members and Mother fed me a great deal of European-type religion. They did not believe in anesthesia, which was important because one day, I slipped off an icy step and bit off a piece of my tongue. The doctor came to the house and sewed it back on without anesthesia. And I did not cry. Mother learned Jewish ways of living from the family she worked for and I suspect she passed along some of those to us.

As I began to learn then, and which was driven home in later years, the basics for anyone considering leaving the crowd so as to be an Isolated Individualist, surviving and thriving in life, and entering the marketplace are what I call Mother's Money Methods. The gist, taught to me as a boy and supplemented by learning the hard way, include the following:

WISE BUYING: "Buy only what is absolutely necessary." "If you really need it, then pay cash." This helped me the most. After working hard to save the money to buy what "I simply could not do without," by the time I had saved the required money, the "need" for the thing had often passed. If you learn about class and what is classy, many of those overpriced clothes can be bought relatively inexpensively in garment districts. The same applies to other accoutrements of daily living.

WISE SAVINGS: Have an ultimate goal for the use of your money. For me, it was a college education. At home, we never threw away any food and made use of all broken and worn out things — rehabilitating them into new uses or for parts to repair other things.

BE CREATIVE: Barter to get the best books and the best teachers.

SAVING MONEY: When you get paid, "first pay yourself 30% of your paycheck and put it in the bank (or someplace similar where it can make money for you"). Education accounts usually pay higher interests than other types of "Mattress" accounts. I never want to put my principal at risk.

WISELY INVEST MONEY: Do not invest in anything requiring all the money you have; and do not ever invest in anything you do not understand.

HAVE EMERGENCY MONEY: Always have hidden and secret money available for emergencies and replace it immediately. Do not let anybody know you have it. Only in emergencies is it okay to spend more than you make. In traveling, I used to carry a money belt.

WISE DEBTS: Pay whatever it takes to obtain a superior education (i.e., developing your talents and skills) related to your career, for this breaks the vicious cycle of poverty and is the way to rise above poverty. When the opportunity arises, "Buy your own home." Start with one you can afford and replace it when you are able. This establishes you as a solid citizen.

It is wise to buy a duplex and rent out one side to reliable people (and not friends). If you are handy, buy a "fixer-upper" and sell it later.

STOP BEING CHEATED OUT OF MONEY: When it comes to money, the overwhelming majority of people cheat. Being hypocritical was normal for medieval knights while cheating, stealing, lying, and other sins were honored by 15th century Europeans. There is no realm where you will not be cheated — the government, banks, attorneys, gasoline stations. Do not trust other people to handle your money. It is important to know how salespersons get paid. Do not have a business charge you for cashing your check. Throughout my life, anything of great material value has been stolen or destroyed or thrown away either by dishonorable or by ignorant people. People are always eager to "borrow" money and always have a "hard luck" story — as in facing eviction or dealing with somebody's death. I have fallen for this maybe 200 times because in one case it may be true. However, I have never been paid back and always lost the friendship of those I have helped the most. Such has happened so often and caused such deep emotional pain that in recent years I have developed the Prophylactic self-protective measure of "Non-Attachment" — meaning that I recognize Tangible losses as a fact of life and choose not to get so attached as to allow it to bother me any longer than six weeks. What I learned is to accept each of those situations as if they are presented to serve as a test. Then I handle each in a manner that makes me stronger. This "That's the Way it is" attitude of acceptance has been very valuable in helping me evolve (see Johns Hopkins).

> "WHEN A CLASSMATE FELL IN THE YARD, I WOULD RUN TO HELP, RATHER THAN JOIN THE OTHER KIDS CROWDING AROUND TO LAUGH."

The Minnesota schools were superb. During my partial first grade education in Minnesota we had learned many, many things — e.g., about the stars and planets, art, carpentry, etc. — which made me enjoy learning. In building a chest of drawers, my experiences with living in the Depression molded the fact of me always having a little extra, just in case. For example, in sawing wood, I would do so on the side where there was some "extra". This "having a spare" or "a little extra" has stayed with me to this day in various forms. At age 5, I was the leader of two gangs of similar 5-year-olds at the same time — Norwegians and Swedes (there were no Black youth that I ever saw) — and both came to my back door every morning. The Swede next door to me was my best friend and he was in the gang to the right of my back door. But, in the 'left gang', the dad of the Norwegian, "Bumpy," owned a candy store. Hence, which gang to lead, my first life's dilemma, was solved by alternating. I would orchestrate the stealing of rhubarb — a bitter celery-like stalk from people's gardens. I am sure they did not really care since it had no particular use for them. Besides, I would send someone to the front door to engage them in conversation while we looted in the back. One of my friend's parents would store apples in a big barrel for the winter but would never let their children eat any that were not spoiling. I sort of formed an impression that despite seeing the point, this is not the best way to enjoy life.

An introduction to Marketplace Indifference devastating to my concerns came as a 5-year-old accustomed to paying a penny for 20 ginger snaps (a thin brittle cookie). Suddenly, because of inflation, the amount was cut to 10 for a penny. I still feel the pangs of this.

My first awareness of contact with my Spiritual Entourage was at age 5 while sitting on the floor of the back porch counting my marbles. Suddenly, the message came that it was time to plan out my life and the Mission was to "Help Bright Black Boys"— a remarkable thing because I was living in Minnesota and never saw any Black People there. Whereas I decided on 5 categories of achievements, my Mission was a "Secret (Sacred) Dream" which I never told anyone about for fear they would laugh at me. I have subsequently achieved them all except living on a farm. From that point on, I never got off course and pursuing those Mission ingredients became the "WE" part of my "ME/WE" orientation to life. To illustrate my continued focus, this book is for them, even though they do not yet know it — and perhaps not for another 50 years.

My Mission category was introduced to me in kindergarten. When a classmate fell in the yard, I would run to help, rather than join the other kids crowding around to laugh. It showed as Compassion, an attribute of Unconditional Love. All life Missions are in the categories of one of the Spiritual Elements.

Becoming aware of this Mission was essential because unknowingly it oriented me to the existence of a Cosmic Organism — that my job was to help improve a tiny piece of it — and both automatically put my life in order. I believe it was open to me because Mother always emphasized aspects of my birth gift which was about being born Selfhood Great. For example, she would say daily: "Son, you can be anything you want to be but always be the best at it as you see it." I misunderstood, thinking she meant I could do "everything" I wanted within that context — and that is what I strove for. But it caused me to me to be very "picky" about what I wanted — and that meant letting go of things I really liked but that were not as important as top priority.

The combination of my Compassion and my Mission message laid the path for me to go into Medicine in order to cultivate my Compassion so that it could teach me about the Unconditional Love demanded for my Mission. As a child, it was a big deal to do whatever it took for me to be able to care for myself in old age because I had seen in outside situations how no one could be depended upon — and having a sense I would be an Isolated Individualist, this meant I would have to be the one to take care of me. Nevertheless, once I had taken care of having "Enough" money to be comfortable in my old age and "extra" to handle health and other problems, my Compassion led me to stop my practice prematurely so as to begin my Mission.

In my retirement, I had no idea that so much money would be needed for things falling apart or deteriorating (e.g., house repairs, like the roof leaking). During this process, a key has been to maintain Integrity. For example, I passed up many opportunities to make illegal money because it simply was not right. Besides, to have gotten caught could have led me to jail. Just after starting the first grade Mother told my sister, Joselyn and me that we were moving to Wilson, North Carolina. Lorenzo Jones, the son of the mother with whom we were living — both Black Americans, told us White people hated Colored people "for no reason." Thus, I would have to protect myself from them. So, I started lifting weights every day in order to get strong for the battle.

WILSON, NORTH CAROLINA: Relatives of Mother in Wilson were Mama Clara, Aunt Julia, and Aunt Cherry who lived at 373 E. Nash Street in this all-Black community. Mother never said how they were related. I suspect it was from my Grandmother, Hattie, a tall Black woman, who had given birth to Mother and my Uncle Cecil in Florence, South Carolina by a Jewish colonel.

I have tried to gain more information from a genealogist and relatives but to no avail. Mother would tell me how she and Grandmother, who lived 10 miles away from the Jewish colonel, for whom Grandmother worked, would get to the train station at 4:00 am to board the 9:00 am train. This was a lesson to tell me to be on time by getting there ahead of time.

When I arrived from Minnesota, on my first morning at school, two Black girls separately came up to me while I was standing in the hall and said: "You think you are better than me!" My response was: "What???" Actually, I had a sound sense of being 'Selfhood Great' but with absolutely no thoughts of being better than anybody or inferior to anyone.

This was the beginning of becoming painfully and immediately aware of how my peers had been beaten down by racism — i.e., losing their inborn sense of Selfhood Greatness. That awareness started the crystallizing of my Mission. Whereas they believed all the evilness they heard from White society, I believed none of it. I saw nothing White people had that was of benefit to me — except their privileges — no standards to which I should aspire and no "just because" compassion displays. They had nothing I wanted and they never seemed to be happy or even satisfied with anything. Actually, they seemed in general like a mean, angry bunch — and, in fact, the ultimate in evilness. Such was clearly and easily and almost daily illustrated by White terrorists, surrounding the Black community, being in the habit of killing Black People on a whim.

By contrast, Black People were simply wonderful — full of community Spiritual Elements — manifestations of Unconditional Love, Truth, Reality, and the Natural. In contrast to my Minnesota experience, after moving to Wilson, North Carolina, I

> "HAVING MANY JOBS AS A BOY AT THE SAME TIME TAUGHT ME ORGANIZATION; HOW TO GET PAID; AND THAT THE JOB HAD TO BE DONE "PERFECTLY" REGARDLESS OF MY DESIRE TO DO SO."

was not able to fit in with my peers. I even put forth the time, energy, and effort to try to imitate what they did (e.g., "acting ugly" in class) and eventually gave up when there were no benefits. Even at that point I had a hint that to love myself and to promote my Selfhood Greatness meant not doing any purposeful harm to myself and not allowing others to do it, if at all possible. Instead, it was simply more comfortable and natural for me to be who I really am — and besides, I have always enjoyed my own company.

Those 3 years in Wilson, living with Mama Clara, Aunt Julia, and Aunt Cherry, was the single most important social event of my life, since here I saw Unconditional Love in action. Mother had gone to Greensboro to get teaching credentials. After a year, she brought my sister there and left me in Wilson. The Wilson family never raised their voices at each other or even argued. If one was getting up to get something, the other would say: "Sit down, I'll get it." Cherry guided my discipline through humor and mind games. Mama Clara and I spent much time in the kitchen because, back then, it was one Black woman's job to be "the cook"— whether at home or in working for White people. She emphasized doing a "perfect" job in pulling the strings off string beans. I would see her kill one of the chickens by chopping the head off and then the headless chicken would run around wildly. That always impressed me. Aunt Julia was my second grade teacher. At home she taught me penmanship — endless rings of circles and up-and-down lines in accordion fashion. Her writing was artful. In her class, she would call out my name and I would respond: "I'm not doing anything." She responded: "That's the problem." A similar display of the Spiritual Elements in action — and never a contradiction within my family — was also present in my all-Black community. That combination became my concept of Beauty — a Beauty associated with Quietness, Gentleness, and Respect for all people. One reason this experience was so profoundly important is that it introduced me to many fundamentals of African Tradition. For example, if I did something wrong and was 10 minutes away from home, by the time I got home, Mama Clara, Aunt Julia, and Aunt Cherry were standing at the door waiting to find out my version of what I had just done. The remarkable thing is that we did not have a telephone. The point: the community helped rear each child. Before being aware of Ancient African Philosophy of Life (POL), I was on that path, starting at age 6. Mrs. Dobbs, my AME Zion Church Sunday School teacher, was a spellbinding storyteller and she loved us kids to death. Her son, Willie Dobbs, was my friend. While having a class in the basement of the Church, she looked in my eyes and made the profound statement: "God is Love and God is within you!" That stunned me to the point of it becoming the seed for my POL. My immediate statement was: "I must learn what Unconditional Love is and how to apply it."

GREENSBORO, NORTH CAROLINA: Upon moving to Greensboro, to join my Mother and Sister, my community sense of African Tradition continued. Inside this warm all-Black community, there was fellowship among all of us, with everybody taking care of everybody else. In times of trouble, there were always several people in the house cleaning up, cooking, or doing whatever needed to be done to help the person get out of trouble or to make things a bit easier if there was no way out. These patterns were a reflection of Ancient African Bible messages having been culturally transmitted, even during African American slavery — and I heard them from the ex-Slaves who were my newspaper customers. All of this was powerful in fashioning my Philosophy of Life (POL). While in the 4th grade, my Dad came to Sam Vick School and, without saying anything, took me to South Carolina and to Arkansas. In Columbia, I met my paternal grandmother, Ophelia. We sat on her front porch with her in her favorite rocking chair and me at her feet. She told me of a relative who wrote the next most famous song to the *Star Spangled Banner* — *America the Beautiful*. Her every sentence ended with "don't you know." My grandfather, John Watson Bailey, owned a grocery store in the middle of a White neighborhood in Columbia, South Carolina. It was probably my grandfather who told me every day that he went to work wearing a starched white shirt with a high collar and bow tie.

He took "no stuff" off anybody and was known to throw White "ruffians" out of his store if they showed any disrespect toward anyone. Today's Black people can gain more respect by showing solidarity in where they choose to spend their money. In Pine Bluff, we lived in a house on campus and Dad was very strict — using a razor strap (a flexible strip of leather) to spank me because of such things as leaving the door open. I understood later why when while playing outside, I came close to a big rattler — which he killed with his gun. I would get eggs out of the chicken coop. At summer's end he sent me back to Greensboro with a family and the male driver was very mean. He would not stop for me to go to the restroom and thus I had to urinate on myself. All I had to eat were the peanut butter and jelly sandwiches which my Dad had prepared — and they were moldy by the last third of the trip. The people put me out on the campus of A & T College and I wandered around until someone recognized me and sent for my Mother — who was in school there as a student and as "Miss A & T".

As a boy, much of my time was spent in a Nature setting. There was quite a bit of lying on my back making cartoons out of looking at the formation of clouds — playing in the snow — gardening — and fishing. It was as a gardener for 10 years that I saw patterns of Nature reproduced in all sorts of ways — which I later learned was a display of the powerful Law of Correspondence.

After a heavy rain, I would rush outside to watch rain water roll down a hill and branch. That taught me how the same things — like a flow of thoughts can be in different forms and yet have the same ingredients. It was also a microcosm of the macrocosm of the Divine Logos. In gardening, there was a similar pattern from seeing how the planting of an apple seed gave rise to roots, a stem, branches, leaves, and eventually fruit — the Icon Image of the Tree Concept method I use to assess and handle problems — by always discerning and starting with the Seed. In doing these things with my dog, Sandy, it gave me the concept of "ME/WE"— that whatever I did for "ME" naturally had to include Sandy, the "WE".

By us walking 3 miles to a fishing place that was just for us, I would take the safety pin, the cork I would get from a wine bottle, and the string and put them together. After picking up a fallen branch and digging in the ground for worms, I would start fishing. To compete with the fish that would bite meant I had to intently watch for the cork to bob the first time. By those fish being no bigger than my boyhood hand, the bob was very slight. Unknown to me at that time, such a focus on the cork taught me to concentrate my attention which, in turn, was an easy way to learn how to discipline my mind to focus instantly. No other tool has been so invaluable in application to other areas of my life. For example, in later life, when bogged down with overwhelming problems and unable to sleep, I would get up in the middle of the night and focus on solving problems of the day.

These were all seeds for my future developing thought structures. Meanwhile, I needed to work and save money to help the family. From then on throughout my pre-college days, I always had at least four jobs at one time — e.g., cutting grass for pay; carrying the local morning and afternoon newspaper, selling *the Afro-American* and *Journal and Guide* — both Black newspapers, working with an electrician, shining shoes, selling my Dad's *New Vista Magazine*, and doing things for elderly neighbors. The most important job was gardening for the family and there would be so much extra that I would share vegetables with neighbors and do gardening for the elderly — both free of charge. People, like Ruth Smith, would laugh at the fact that I could never grow a straight row of beans — and they called that "Drunk Beans." Having many jobs as a boy at the same time taught me organization: how to get paid; and that the job had to be done "perfectly" regardless of my desire to do so.

From that I learned not to have likes and dislikes about things needing to be done but, instead, be immediately about doing it. These were transferrable skills that made it alright to "do a mile of work to make an inch of progress." I also liked "doing all I can; the best I can; as fast as I can; and as long as I can" because each of those aspects was a constant challenge. How problems were handled during those bad times helped develop a strong character in me. Meanwhile, White terrorists continued the habit of killing Black People on a whim.

Although it was a fun challenge to see if I could do things perfectly, I never applied these standards to others. There was little time to socialize with my peers because of my work obligations. Most socialization came from making fun out of hard work and really enjoying being a Boy Scout. In earning the 24 merit badges to qualify for my Eagle award, one was "Life Saving" in water. My

> "NOTHING HAS BEEN MORE PROMINENT IN BLACK PEOPLE'S TRADITION IN AFRICA AND IN MY BOYHOOD THAN HAVING GOOD MANNERS — AND IT BEGINS ALL TRAINING FOR WORLD SUCCESS."

instructor told me to tread water for 15 minutes and I answered: "I can't do that." He: "Did I hear you say Can't? — then do it 30 minutes!" Me: "I know I can't go that long." He: "Did I hear you say Can't? — then do it 45 minutes!" By then I had learned the lesson and jumped in the pool. After treading water 45 minutes, I never said what I Can't do again. Meanwhile, the Whites in charge of the Boy Scouts did not want a Black youth to have that award and therefore "lost" all my records. My parents threatened to sue them in Federal Court and so they allowed me to re-earn the 24 merit badges and get the Eagle award. In the process, there was a Boy Scout Jamboree in Santa Ana, California, and to be able to attend, I had to sell my 1934 Ford (with its rumble seat in the back) and borrow $25 from Smitty (which I promptly paid back a month later). But the Boy Scout leaders would not allow me to ride in the same train car with the White Scouts and thus I rode alone. Oddly, a group of White boys used to like to come play tackle football with us every Saturday morning. I would hit the guy I was tackling with all the strength I could muster. Yet, I did not hate them or anyone — ever! We always won.

Further crystallization of my Mission occurred from seeing huge numbers of my high school classmates — some simply brilliant; some with world class talent — drop out of school and head directly into "dead ends." This was so painful for me that I vowed then to make myself a success and return to do all I could to help Black youth free their Enslaved Minds. But this required carving out my own path alone. Fortunately, I had the personal experience of being in the middle of the finest display of good Manners and civility in my life. This was in my boyhood days, in the Black community of Wilson and Greensboro, North Carolina. My wonderful all-Black environment gave me a sense of Manners (being quite concerned about the feelings of others) and an Ancient African orientation to *Ma'at* living (e.g., to maintain Integrity and honorableness at all costs). Afrocentric Manners are about dealing with things of Worth — i.e., the Spiritual Elements and their attributes (which are like "the Sun and its rays") all being "Involved" (i.e., wrapped up together) when approaching others so they can become "Evolved" (unwrapped in manifesting) in harmonious displays. That harmony makes for complete adaptation of each part to the whole, implying perfect adjustment of all conditions — and this experience of Worth, which gives one an inner sense of Order and Balance, is true on all planes of existence — e.g., mental, physical, and spiritual. Ancient Africans considered Worth to be concerned with qualities dealing with Spiritual Enlightenment (the highest level of spiritual awakening) and Immortality — even being more significant than Harmony and Peace. This may or may not embrace whatever is of Value. Value concerns the Explicit — Scarce Desirables of the Material World that provide benefits seen in more ways than just itself.

The Implicit Beauty of a Thing and/or what is significant for its own sake as a result of simply having come into Being within the Cosmic Organism is what expands one's "ME/WE" Consciousness and enhances one's Character. A mannerly way Character is reflected is in caring for the Dignity (i.e., being made in God's image), Divinity, and feelings present in others. Examples: making others feel good; not doing anything to offend them; and/or assisting them to feel less bad. Nothing has been more prominent in Black People's tradition in Africa and in my boyhood than having Good Manners — and it begins all training for world success. It is a terrible thing for me to see that this has been all but wiped out by Black People following Europeans' behaviors and trends. Most prominent is in not responding to people who do things for them selflessly along with ignoring people in positions of power that can help them self-improve personally and in the public realm. Even if one has never been taught what good manners are (and there are plenty of ways to learn them), simply give thought to "What is in the best interest of my mate that I can do now?" and then carry it out. When it comes to Value (that which has a high price tag for the market place — a lot of money or possessions, status, power over people, or fame), true respect is the giving of the proper amount of honor due to the person for his/her honorable accomplishments. Such persons deserve even greater respect if they are Black and have used their accomplishments for the betterment of Humankind.

What was particularly powerful was talking with ex-Slaves who were my newspaper customers. Since they had never been allowed to develop their Intellect, they had perfected their pre-birth Emotions — those connected to the Cosmic Organism of all God's creatures and creations prior to being born into the Earth world. Expressions of pre-birth Emotions (or Feelings) are about being plain and simple — about Harmony and Beauty — about respecting the Dignity or Substance of God in everything real and not evil — about Wisdom in practical living. They did not talk much but none of it was about hate or revenge but rather directly on the bull's eye of an archery pad of the best ways to live. For example, one elderly lady said: "Seek the Truth and build all of your decisions around it." From all of this, I had a concept of Common Sense (from the ex-Slaves) — and how to use it to convert filtered Information into Knowledge. Also, the proper application of pertinent Knowledge at the right time and in the right Spiritual Elements flow and Manners was the way to develop Wisdom. Throughout my boyhood, I had always heard from the Black Community: "What college are you going to?"—and never, "Are you going to college?" There was an atmosphere of educational improvement.

At age 13, I made a decision to let people go, from a social orientation perspective, because I needed to do certain things in preparation for my Mission in life — and that took every spare moment. This shifted me away from focusing on interests of the Crowd — other people's business and events and fashions or fads over to dealing with ideas related to self-improvement and personal defense for the "alligators" I would have to face. People simply took too much of my time. But I promised that when I was comfortable I would come back to socialize. However, a half century apart meant that they and I had gone down such diverging paths that we were no longer in shouting distance for communication. This life-changing decision of going away from people meant losing contact with how they thought, felt, expressed themselves, and behaved. That automatically reduced my desires to have a lot of new "Stuff". Also, they developed ideas about me based on what was familiar to them, which had, in reality, nothing to do with me. Thus, I did not like people to know what I was doing or how because they would jump to wrong conclusions about it. In addition, I had great Pain at seeing bright and talented Black peers enter dead-end paths — and that pain gave reinforcement to pursue my Mission and discover ways to make it happen. One classmate was shot and killed over a nickel.

My great ambition, at this point, was boundless and it needed self-improvement. To this end, besides learnings related to my education, training, and experience, I was also looking for principles useful for teaching or sharing with those who might be interested. I learned to entertain myself (fortunately, there was no television or Flashing Light gadgets) by reading things designed to show me ways to live life well and with enjoyment. My favorites were works of Will Rogers, Mark Twain, Ben Franklin, and George Washington Carver (among others). I was addicted to all types of silly jokes and one-liner proverbs (e.g., For every minute of sadness, you give up 60 seconds of happiness"). With never a thought of trying to get out of work, I would eagerly take on work and strive to do it perfectly. I would eagerly get my work done as fast as I could so as to help others do their jobs. In this way, I learned about new problems and ways to handle and not handle them. A payoff was getting more work to do that was at a more difficult level. Vital to this was learning how to make fun out of hard work, fashion small successes every day, like making my bed without wrinkles, and doing the foundational for maintaining a sense of Selfhood Greatness by doing each job so perfectly, by my standards — and even if no one saw it — as to be overwhelmed with Self-Pride.

Guidelines along this path demanded seeking and staying with the Truth, Reality, and personal Integrity. But doing so involved a great deal of "trial and error" as well as increasing my awareness of the details of what I believe to be right (mainly by reading Ancient African POL). Yet, because I love myself and do not believe in doing things that do not benefit "ME/WE," I have never done anything to intentionally harm anyone or myself because I believe both are fundamental to cultivating one's Unconditional Love. Such embraces my never having hated anyone. Staying angry is not beneficial.

I had pangs of wanting to follow the Crowd. One was when many classmates dropped out of school to go into the military to serve in the Korean War — and many got killed. My Mother would have no part of me doing that. Grown men returning to James B. Dudley High School were on the football team. I tried out for it but there was "no contest" once I started running into men 50% heavier than me. As a result, I became the manager and got to go on all the trips. I wrote an article for the high school newspaper every time it came out, under the direction of my Mother, who taught English. I liked to buy an ice cream sandwich at lunch time, stick it in my pocket, and then hide in the back of the class and eat it. But by the time that happened, ice cream was running all down my leg. I had a terrible time with language and would have Grace Dungee do her French assignments with a carbon copy. Though I am not certain I did this, when I did not have time to copy it I turned in the carbon!

In typing class I liked to listen to the radio when the Brooklyn Dodgers were playing. We boys were all obsessed with Jackie Robinson, Roy Campanella, and Don Newcombe. So, I had a friend put a jack on the radio that would fit the plug on my typing ear phones. My typing was like Russian. Whereas White students had grown professional school bus drivers, the school board used student drivers for the Black youth. I was the only one who ever had an accident by driving under a port at a service station and breaking the light bulb. Black students were never given new books but rather the used books of White students. It was my job to unwrap those books; it would make me angry every time I took each book out of the box. We were never taught any Black History, except in the 4th grade — and that consisted of a picture of Little Black Sambo, with a bone through his nose, being chased around a tree by a lion. We alternated between USA and North Carolina history each year and nothing has ever bored me more. I never believed "how great Whites are" or what was claimed they did because my Black community let me know these falsely claimed achievements had been stolen from Black People, like the cotton gin. This history contributed to me flunking all of my senior year courses, and my Mother was one who gave me an "F".

Meanwhile, all I was exposed to in my formal education was European information and for years I thought this was worthwhile — because it was the only thing to which I was exposed. Nevertheless, the European information did not ring true — partly because it was disharmonious and mainly because much of what I learned in school made no sense (e.g., philosophy). I assumed that since there was nothing taught about Black People, that the European information was not important — mainly because it was not applicable to my life. Why should I care about what Henry VIII of England did? I was so bored, I flunked my senior year in high school. But fortunately, I had already been accepted to the University of Michigan. Of great importance in high school was Industrial Arts where I learned to use the right tool for the job — keep that tool in good working condition — and clean it and put it back in its proper place once I had finished with it. Putting things back as I found them was vital in striving to be efficient. I cared about saving parts of anything I used after reading the book "Cheaper By The Dozen."

My parents were extremely active in the community — responsible for a number of things getting done for Black People — a YWCA; Affordable Housing Affairs. Even White people did not disrespect my Mother (addressing her as "Mrs. Smith") and when she died, the flag was flown at half-mast in her honor. Smitty, my step-dad, was Dean of Trades at A & T and the college named a building after him and Mother. He was a great man — half Cherokee Indian and half African. He introduced me to tools and the proper care of them — as in keeping them sharp and putting them back in their place when one finished with them. Putting things back like you found them was also emphasized by my Mother, as it had been in Industrial Arts at Dudley. This is a great habit to get into because it saves valuable time when staying on point is necessary so as to not disrupt the flow.

UNIVERSITY OF MICHIGAN: I chose the University of Michigan because Smitty had gone there. When I left home to attend the University of Michigan, an immediate shock was going into an atmosphere where nobody cared about me or even spoke to me. Hence, I was left completely on my own to survive, or not. The first few days I had terrible stomach pains which were diagnosed at the Infirmary as "Distress". All of this instantly made me both Isolated and an Individualist in having to figure out how to do everything for myself. It differed from Europeans' emphasis on individualism because, whereas despite disliking each other, they form alliances to meet what they deem to be a common foe (typically gentle and peaceful Black People who had things they wanted and who are tremendously envied), I had no one to turn to or with whom I could talk so as to relieve tension. This hostile and essentially all-White environment was a situational state I had never seen nor heard of before. This is when my Spiritual Entourage made their presence known by sending me "Helping Hands" — but by not being aware they existed meant I did not use them fully to my advantage. It was necessary for me to self-educate (i.e., go within myself and draw out what is there). What these Europeans taught made no sense to me, for it was in a Supernatural world, not the Spiritual environment in which I grew up.

At no time did I see White students having a really good time, as I had seen Black youth do. All acted as if they knew everything — all in areas unknown to me. Yet, I outscored most of my classmates. In Chemistry, I was so far behind that the first and only time I went to talk with the teacher, she gave profound advice: "Start where you are!" Up to that point I had been failing and then discovered it was because I had never been told what was the "Big Picture" of the subject. I got an idea of that by mid-semester and thereafter got A's. The only course meaningful to me was that of Greek and Latin word origins — important for later medical school, for all types of research and writings, and for learning that the stories of English, Greek, and Latin words all led back to Africa. It let me know that Ancient Africans have the highest of Knowledge + Wisdom + Truth and that Europeans have none of these — and have no way to get to them. My Selfhood Greatness sense was even more riled up in keeping me from believing anything White people said. I was in ROTC (Reserve Officer Training Corps) and was squadron leader. I learned about European time. Since my only exposure was to European information, for years I thought this was somehow worthwhile — even though much of what I learned in school was "over my head" (e.g., philosophy). In recent years, I realized their "big words" and strange concepts lack reality meaning — only reflecting mere Supernatural fantasies geared to mind control. That is the reason why European education is so inferior for Blacks. Now, I would not change it because it made me a stronger person — sharpening my focus on and dedication to my goals.

MOREHOUSE COLLEGE: As a boy, in preparation for college, I always had at least 4 jobs at one time — saving my money for college. It amounted to $8,000 and I thought that was enough to do everything and that it would last forever. My money ran out in two years and I transferred to the all-Black Morehouse College in Atlanta, Georgia because my Dad had gone there. "My G's" — i.e., "my Guys" — had a proper concept of work, play, and family — called "Apportionment". I had no sooner unpacked when a group of students came to tell me the Morehouse way of apportioning time as a way to fashion a System, Plan, and Regular procedure. Apportionment is illustrated by drawing a picture of a big pie and determining how large the slices will be in order for one to account for every single thing one has to do within a 24-hour day. For example, they said Saturday morning is when to get personal things in order (e.g., washing and ironing clothes; writing letters to family); Saturday afternoon is getting prepared for the next week's courses; late Saturday evening is going out on the town; Sunday morning is Chapel Time; Sunday afternoon is spent with "your lady"; and the rest of the week is spent in classrooms and study. But after supper the practice was to take a thin slice of the apportionment pie to spend time with friends. What I took away was that the best use of time, energy, and effort is to have a place for everything with everything in its place. Then do the easiest first when dealing with "Impossible" problems (Bailey, *Leadership Critical Thinking*); the most important first when there is limited time; or what is alphabetical or chronological in trying to establish Order.

Since I was completely "broke," I revitalized my boyhood hobby of photography and started taking portrait pictures for a dollar a piece. Business got so good as to interfere with my studies. So I raised my fee to four dollars a picture — and business boomed. By having planned ahead in working and saving money while my teenage peers played, the "asides" I learned turned out to be what kept me going — without losing a beat. By contrast, very poor people's daily lives are spent simply trying to survive the day. Thus, they do not have the opportunity to save and engage in "asides." No longer did I have to eat grits three meals a day; I could now go to restaurants. I learned life-shaping things there — as to study Principles. The most outstanding thing was that Morehouse emphasized learning Principles, and we would study one for a week, looking at it like it was a box with sides and angles that were essential to its make-up. Another fundamental came from trial and error and without intent. One "Tool" learning situation pertained to being dissatisfied with how I was taking notes and being uncertain as to what form to store them. As a result of re-copying them several times — first on paper, then a softback notebook, then a hardback binder, etc., I learned what was important to remember.

The day I switched from listening to classical music to Jazz was when a "dapperly" dressed "G" — complete with vest and bow tie — came into my room carrying a package wrapped by a ribbon. All of the "G's" in the room got completely quiet because they were fascinated. With deliberate drama, Mr. Dapper unwrapped the package to display a record album in a way for us to see it cost $4.99! Other "G's" had only ever paid $0.99 for their records. I had never bought one but I had the only record player — obtained from a guy who used it in barter since he had had a lot of pictures taken by me. Once I heard "Opus d' Jazz," by the Modern Jazz Quartet, I was transformed. That night, I packed all of my classical records and sent them to my sister. But as an Isolated Individualist, it was essential to have Plans B and C as "back-ups," along with reserves needed to prevent a loss of momentum. To illustrate, although I never wavered from desiring to be a physician (driven by a strong sense of Compassion, first noticed as a small boy), in case I did not get into medical school, I was prepared to go into medical photography. That was spurred by my boyhood photography hobby coupled with a natural attraction to medicine. Throughout my entire education, training, and experience there was no place where anger, blame, or revenge would benefit my progress. Hence, they were dropped instantly because I needed to be clear in mind to stay awake and alert to dangers and to opportunities.

MEHARRY MEDICAL SCHOOL: Upon arriving at Meharry, I had a small apartment and only $96 to furnish it. So, I picked up throw-away furniture on the streets and bought a used refrigerator and stove. With the $25 dollars left, I bought a Ford with big red and blue flames on both sides. It gave me so much trouble that one day, while downtown waiting for a traffic light, I got out — left it running and walked home. I never saw it or heard about it again. The principle is to drop what is an unnecessary problem. In contrast to the University of Michigan, my Morehouse education was so good that it was 6 months into Meharry Medical School (Nashville, Tennessee) before I began to encounter new information. There, I did nothing more than go to class, study, and work to pay tuition and other expenses. A price I could not help paying for failing to socialize with classmates was to be left out of practically all of their extra-curricular activities. However, achieving my Mission was the top priority. I learned to arrive in class 5 minutes early, take a front row seat where the speaker was most clearly seen, and become skilled at taking notes (because what the instructor gave was what she/he thought was most important). I did not have much money; I had a job which paid just enough for rent. Thus, I bought a House Trailer and bargained with a family in the community who had a vacant lot to rent and would allow me to tap into their electricity and sewage. The total cost was still less than I had been paying. But then, expenses went up and I had to get rid of the Trailer, since Mother said she would not loan me the money. I practically gave it away to a physician and lived in a basement room. I offered to share it with a classmate and he came in and took the favorite spot. I accepted this because I needed his share of the rent money. But for a while, it was the Good Life.

I had two German Shepherd dogs — and the one with the pedigree was really dumb. I had an old DeSoto car and the tires were bald when I got it. In driving home to Greensboro, I had to take the long way so as to be close to a running stream of water. The reason was it would run hot about every 15 miles. Still, the bald tires held up. During the summer vacation following my Freshman year, I was selected to be an Extern at Riverside Seventh Day

Adventist Hospital. There, I was introduced to assisting during surgeries. My first surgery taught me about planning ahead. I failed to go to the restroom before starting and that operation lasted 7+ hours — with me being "miserable" the entire time of the "Whipple" operation. I also learned it takes a will to live. A 60-year-old lady admitted to the hospital asked me to call her sister and tell her that she, the patient, was going to die at midnight. I did a thorough work-up and found nothing wrong. I checked on her every few minutes. When I went in at midnight, she was dead. An autopsy found no specific cause of death. Another summer, I was accepted at a New York Hospital where there were multi-deformed children. After a day of assisting in operating, I could not tolerate something about it and left for St. Louis where I Externed at Homer G. Phillips Hospital. The patients were mainly alcohol addicts, especially to "Sweet Rosey O'Grady" alcohol. I could sew body parts back on without anesthesia while they kept singing.

So many had pancreatitis that I could give complete orders at 3:00 am while trying to awaken from a deep sleep. I thought I could never forget those orders but 6 months later I could remember none. Thereafter, I learned to always write down in my self-created "Dictionary" anything important, no matter how automatic it was to me. My last summer, I was selected to go to Sloan-Kettering Cancer Hospital in New York City where I learned some of the finer points of surgery. Slowly, I was beginning to get the "Big Picture" of medicine and made the Dean's List. I had liked Orthopaedics taught by Dr. Dooley. I had scrubbed for him and one day he asked me to go to his car to get something. When I got on the elevator, I dropped his car keys between the crack in the elevator floor so that they went down the shaft to the bottom. It was a big deal to find out how to get them and even worse telling him what happened. That helped me to be more careful. On the final exam, he told the class that the name of the textbook: *Handbook For Orthopaedics* by Dr. Compere would be on the exam and anybody who got it wrong would drop a grade point. I got it wrong and wound up with a B. Oddly, when I first went into practice, I was there to assist Dr. Compere at El Monte Medical Center in Los Angeles. I remained appreciative of Meharry and send her money each year. She has my 40 books and 700 of my Black History articles on line for library students to use.

LOS ANGELES COUNTY HOSPITAL: On my last day at Meharry, I was standing in the hall trying to decide if I should accept my Internship for Los Angeles County Hospital or stay at Meharry. Then a pathologist I did not like walked past. Thus, I instantly selected LA County. That was a good choice because I liked the city and they paid $180 a month — more than any other hospital in the USA. But there, like everywhere, the hours were cruel — 36 hours on and 12 off. There was no sitting down on work hours because things were "hopping" everywhere: going from bed to bed delivering babies and, in between, delivering one in the elevator. Once, I was so tired that while sitting and waiting for a baby to come out, I went to sleep. The baby dropped into my lap.

I liked Orthopaedics and had Frank Jobe, the now famous Orthopaedic Surgeon for professional athletes, as my chief resident. He allowed me to do my first amputation — above the knee. The only patient that died was one with asthma. I had treated him for days and with good results. The morning I went to discharge him, the nurse said he had died. The autopsy showed it was from his system being exhausted by the cortisone he had been taking all of his life. There were plenty of parties. But I often preferred to get in my DeSoto and drive to Hermosa Beach. There, at the Light House, I would listen to top jazz musicians practicing for the evening performances — and simply playing for fun was when they were at their best. I knew and visited every jazz club in Los Angeles. There were so many places to go around the clock that often I did not sleep on my 12 hours off. One place on Adams and Crenshaw opened at 5:00 am and I was often there when famous entertainers would come in. One would say: "I left more women in bed than are here." My friend Jervis, a tall blue-eyed blond from Mississippi, would make rounds early and during our off hours, go to silent movies. Since no one was inside, we could laugh and scream while stuffing our mouths with popcorn. He had a Jaguar that typically broke down and that taught me that to maintain expensive things cost a lot of time and money.

I took frequent trips up and down the coast — like to Monterey. Near San Diego, there was a restaurant that looked like an old house. Its back porch faced the ocean and I would spend hours there, sitting and drinking wine. Along the way, I would see houses on the beach for sale at $10,000 and always wondered why people did not buy these right away. One of my traits has been to be ready to move on when the time came and not leave where I was with regret or by looking forward to the future. I found it best to keep my emotions off things that had to be done so as to save that energy for hitting the ground running when figuratively thrown off a roof. Also, I knew to never show my emotions to Europeans, for that is like blood to a shark who then moves in for the attack.

UNITED STATES AIR FORCE: Following Medical Training and Internship at Los Angeles County Hospital, I had no choice but to go into the USA Air Force. A racial incident in San Antonio, Texas involved my classmate and me. Both in uniform with captain emblems in full view, we went into a café to have lunch. We were immediately and rudely refused because "Colored Pe-

> **I HAVE NEVER ALLOWED ANYONE TO DICTATE WHO I SHOULD BE OR WHAT I SHOULD DO. I ASSESS THEM AS HAVING THEIR LIFE IN DISORDER, WHICH ALONE DISQUALIFIES THEM FROM TELLING ME WHAT TO DO.**

ople were not allowed." On account of this, I deliberately failed my examination the next day. Thus, my assignment was switched from Kimpo, Korea to Clark in the Philippines. Three days before my flight, I was told I had 48 hours to get to San Francisco. I was in the process of ordering an Impala — with the antenna sticking out of the back — red lights for the interior — a black interior. I put a rush on it and immediately took off in it — driving day and night. But that was the first time I ever had an air conditioner and it was a great drive. When I got to the airport, I saw someone, gave them $100 dollars and the keys to the car so they could see that the car got on the ship to Clark. Then I went through a line getting all kinds of shots. On the way to the plane, despite being exhausted, I noticed a woman with several kids, struggling with the luggage. I carried some, got on the propeller plane, and collapsed. Then I was awakened by the stewardess asking me if I was a physician. I said no but she said: "Yes you are." A lady had just collapsed — the lady I had helped on the plane — and the pilot was awaiting orders from me as to what to do. Really!!! I had no idea but still barked orders to fly low and stop in Hawaii — which they did. After 17 hours I got to Clark and an extremely talkative captain met me and started telling me all the things lined up for that evening. He would not stop talking all the way to my quarters.

When we got out, there were Negritos sleeping on the rooftop, despite this being the rainy season. I was told that they helped to protect the Base from sniper Japanese who were not aware World War II was over. I went inside, where upon sitting on the bed, I passed out. I was assigned as a general practitioner and later as Captain in medical charge of 10,000 troops. Unfortunately, all of my belongings had been sent to Kimpo and I never saw them again. This was a first lesson in countless others of adopting to never being attached to material things. That was a vital lesson for helping me to stay "on course" to my Mission. By seeing 80 patients a day, rather than the required 20, and then by volunteering after hours to help treat the wounded soldiers flown in from Vietnam, I learned as much as was possible about various aspects of Medicine. This included treating the Negritos, some having "lockjaw" and other strange diseases. In medical school, I had not paid much attention to the "Tropical Diseases" course, thinking I would never have a need for it. Yet, that was what I needed the most — a lesson in me trying to "pick and choose" from a program experts had selected. That is a principle for acquiring Knowledge. My practice included volumes of all types of patients — e.g., gynecology and pediatrics. Here, I learned I could not put up with the demanding mothers and decided then not to go into Pediatrics. The only thing I could not master was Orthopaedics and its mystery was intriguing. That is what caused me to choose to go into Orthopaedic Surgery.

I was stunned by the large number of USAF (United States Air Force) airplane crashes that were never reported. We medical personnel would line the runway for any aircraft reported to be in trouble. One crashed while landing and the 119 soldiers were burnt into charred, pretzel positions — all dead as I went from seat to seat. That is the worst thing I ever saw. The most upset I was came from 3 hard days of work in trying to save the life of a pilot. I brought him back to a lucid state whereby we became friends. I sent him back to a San Francisco Hospital and when I called the next day, I was told he had died. It was appalling how rude the White troops were to the Filipinos — completely putting in disarray the way they had historically done things —

giving the women money in exchange for "favors." This led many of them to "act ugly" with their own Filipino boyfriends and husbands. I lived off Base at Paulino's Motel and became friends with Ray Paulino, a movie producer. He and the starlets used my apartment for lounging between filming. Later, he was shot and killed during a political election. The Filipinos were a gentle, fun-loving people and I enjoyed visiting them at their "fish ponds" — actually lakes. They controlled and disciplined their children with soft, quiet voices.

HAHNEMANN HOSPITAL: At that time, Orthopaedic Surgery was a southern White male dominated specialty and they did not want Black physicians in it. Hence, only one of the nine Black Orthopaedic Surgeons had passed his board examinations and I was determined to be the second — which I was. Upon being accepted, I took a leave from Clark to visit the Hospital. As soon as I put my hand on the handle to open the door to the lounge, I had a bad feeling about that place. Ten days later, I was accepted at Mount Sinai in New York, a top program in the world. But because I had given my word to Hahnemann, I stayed with it. I had ordered an MG from Britain to arrive at Philadelphia when I got there. The day it arrived, I went to the dock and the guy delivering it said: "You will not do this, but 2 years from today get rid of this car." He was right. I really, really enjoyed that car but 2 years later it became a financial cancer. For example, it would not go forward and a few times I had to drive it backwards in order to get home.

Nevertheless, my first day as a resident was in the Emergency room. My chief told me: "I'm going to play golf; do not call me for any reason." Hahnemann was a hospital for treating police. I did such a good job as to be given a card indicating I was an honorary member of the Police — and that card has helped me a great deal.

This meant putting up with a bunch of "bad stuff"; being under the microscope for assessing every little thing I did or did not do so as to have no wiggle room for errors; and doing "good" work was not acceptable, for it had to be excellent. Such spurred me to learn new and faster and better routes for achieving "perfect" outcomes — and in the face of ongoing hostility and obstacles on the path.

This also meant choosing important but untraveled routes in order to make achievements. For example, I started doing research, especially on ancient ways of doing things in Orthopaedic Surgery (since I was forced to deal with "one of a kind" type things in congenital anomalies and since I could get no help from White Orthopaedic Surgeons). To these ends, I learned non-European information that seemed to make sense or at least more sense. As the only brown face, White people resented this but I never had any problem with White patients while being their Physician. It was typical for many of the people with whom I was in contact to constantly try to dump on me. But because of my Self-Declaration to not let anything stop me, I said nothing and did what I was told, despite much of that being unfair. For example, the chief resident did not dictate any of his discharge summaries (a note briefly describing the course of a patient's treatment) and I was told to do it if I intended to stay in the program. It was essential for me to never show any emotions; I maintained my composure in the face of hostility. By ensuring no one could read my face for emotions, this prevented blow ups for which they could cite me and then kick me out of the program. Since they would not give me operating room scrub nurses, I had to learn the jobs of those nurses and teach them to the first-day student nurses assigned to me. Thus, I would ensure that all instruments anticipated needing were laid out on a table and I would instruct the students to hand those in that order. It got so my team was the fastest of them all. I did one femur (thigh bone) fracture in 14 minutes, from "skin to skin"— i.e., from the incision to the last stitch. Soon enough, it dawned on me that I would not be allowed to have the Elizabeth Town Crippled Children's rotation, which was both a prized rotation and necessary for my boards. Fellows from Jefferson Hospital had therefore selected someone to take my place. I spoke with the Chief, and somehow, they let me have that rotation. I was to alternate being on call every other night with a fellow resident but many, many times he failed to show up. That necessitated me being up for 72 hours. Even though the staff was against teaching me, invariably the chief would come in at 8:00 p.m. wanting to make rounds and "teach". I agreed to teach the student nurses and was told that I did a nice job helping them understand difficult things, like Traction-Suspensions. Dr. Green's secretary told me I explained things very well. Anyone associated with me was harassed by the director because the top people assumed and claimed I was trying to marry a White girl, because they are special. Meanwhile, all of the various department heads were engaged in the façade of them being about diversity and education for all, regardless of race, creed, or color. But, to balance this out, the Black workers were all "For me". I would have to rush past the cafeteria during the day going from the clinic to surgery, and not having time to eat. So, on their own, they would fix a lunch bag for me and stand outside to hand it to me as I ran by. The Black elevator operators also looked out for me in various ways. I always maintained a mindset of Selfhood Greatness.

One girlfriend told me that when I walked on the street and met White people, I did not get out of their way, as most Black People did in the South. The reason is that I felt I had as much right to be where I was as anybody in the world and that they had to get out of my way if they were on the wrong side of the walkway. If they came directly at me, I simply stopped and stood my ground. When people judge me, they leave themselves open for me to judge them. I have never allowed anyone to dictate who I should be or what I should do. I assess them as having their life in disorder, which alone disqualifies them from telling me what to do. I have no problem with how they live and have no hatred of evil people. I simply see them as evil and thus I need to avoid them or figure out how to get around them. But if I have to compete with them, then I learn everything they know so as to outsmart them and then outwork them.

ELIZABETH TOWN CRIPPLED CHILDREN'S HOSPITAL: This was a very racist place. No one would rent an apartment to me in the surrounding town and so the hospital gave me one of theirs. In the cafeteria, I would sit at a table, keeping to myself. One day, I was called into the office and the head guy said: "What are you trying to do, start a Little Rock?" (where racism required the National Guard to accompany Black children to school). He sent out a directive that no one was to sit with me in the cafeteria. They assigned me to the Clubfoot Clinic — the one no resident wanted. But I did research to discover the various ways Clubfoot had been treated in the past — took bits and pieces of each way — and created my own version. Soon, I was getting such rapid results that people would come to visit to see what I was doing. This lesson is that "when given a lemon, make lemonade."

I got along extremely well with the children. At times they would cheer when I came in. They gave me so much aftershave that to this day I am still using it, with more in the drawers. On weekends, I would have to drive to Hahnemann to dictate reports that did not belong to me. Since I did not like the disrespect, I decided to change Resident programs. I invented a Heel Cord Stretching Brace for which the brace-maker claimed credit and published it.

HOSPITAL FOR JOINT DISEASES: Because a senior resident had been drafted out of their program, the Hospital for Joint Diseases in New York (1919 Madison Ave.) had an opening and I was accepted — one of the 8 places I integrated. They were sort of neutral towards me and distant but I was there to get an education. These were smart Jews and the chief would tell me which article to read for a case — which was the best. That had never happened at Hahnemann — meaning I would read 99 articles on the subject but not the best one since I was unaware of it. I developed a Traction-Suspension Splint and patented it because it was the first improvement since the Civil War. Dr. Mankin found it very beneficial for his post-operative total hip patients because there was no groin ring. I published that — my second??? *A Towel Sling* was published at Hahnemann — my first. In 1967, as a senior resident, Dr. Milgram, one of the grandfathers of Orthopaedics, had the practice of me not talking while in his presence but to simply listen. While walking through an underground parking lot he suddenly stopped and said: "Do not get involved in the Civil Rights Movements" (I had been a Freedom Rider just prior). After a pause, he added: "Because you need to figure out what course Black people should take once all the rowdy activity is over. Actually, someone should pay you to think." In New York, I went to all types of Jazz clubs. I never locked my car that was parked on the street until someone told me I should. When I did, someone broke in and so I continued to leave it open after that. I felt my training had been inadequate and thus decided to take some extra training in Genetics at Johns Hopkins — for reasons I no longer remember. I told Dr. Milgram and he suggested I not go because "they are still fighting the Civil War." But since they had the best program in the USA, I decided to go anyway. One of my traits has been to be ready to move on when the time came and not leaving with regret or looking forward to the future. I found it best to keep my emotion off things that had to be done so as to save that energy for hitting the ground running.

> "...MY DISCOVERIES WERE IMMEDIATELY CLAIMED BY OTHERS. AS A RESULT OF ALL THE CREDIT BEING GIVEN TO OTHERS, THIS MEANT THAT I WAS ESSENTIALLY IGNORED. THIS HURT ME BECAUSE OF ITS UNFAIRNESS UNTIL I REALIZED MY OVERRIDING OBJECTIVE HAD BEEN ACCOMPLISHED."

JOHNS HOPKINS HOSPITAL: This route was important both for my career in Orthopaedic Surgery as well as for my Mission. I went there to do something significant — something other White Physicians were not doing. This was not about trying to impress anybody or do something I thought I could not do. Rather, it was about demonstrating Unconditional Love to the truly needy — as I saw it — because of problems that were no fault of their own. Shortly after I arrived, the Little People of America had their convention in Baltimore. I had occasion to work with "Little People" — popularly called Dwarfs — on an issue no one in the history of Humankind had been able to untangle. From intensive study, I made discoveries that affected the world. Because I was an Orthopaedic Surgeon who knew how to read X-rays and they had never had a surgeon taking Medical Genetics, I was allowed to examine all 54 (or so) — while the Medical Fellows only examined 6 — and they needed a radiologist to read their X-rays. I then asked all the Fellows at the lunch table if any were working on Dwarfs and, if not, I would. All said they were not and seemingly had no interest. Only later did I realize each was intensely interested. Yet, under the impression of not "stepping on anyone's toes," I worked hard before and after everyone went home. I would travel up to 500 miles to evaluate one Dwarf and spend up to 4 days in a given hospital looking through X-rays, perhaps coming up with one or two cases. Eventually, I had the largest collection in the world — known by having all of the world's literature on the subject translated. Then I could begin to see patterns that enabled me to diagnose a hypoplastic odontoid (the deformed neck bone the head spins on) which accounted for the 4 limb weakness. Up to this point, the Fellows said that 4 limb weakness was normal for them.

Yet, my discoveries showed certain syndromes had such 4 limb weakness and from which many would die once their protecting neck muscles were relaxed under general anesthesia (and thereby compressing their spinal cord). This saved innumerable Dwarfs' lives worldwide. There came a time when I had all members of the Hopkins typing pool typing my papers. People really disliked this and wondered where I was getting all of the information when none was available to them. They went so far as to claim I must be stealing it from somewhere and that caused the chief to close the Hopkins X-ray files to me. I was stunned. One day, around all of this, I was standing in the middle of a 5-points passageway when Steve Kopics, my friend and Orthopaedic Surgeon came up beside me and said: "You must continue your work; nobody else will and nobody can." This was motivating and I published an article in the *Journal of Bone and Joint Surgery* — the leading publication of the world. Although they were rejecting 10,000 submissions a month, they made my article their lead — i.e., the most important. That caused people from all over the world to send me their X-rays and work-ups for diagnoses and suggestions for treatment. As a result, I was able to put a book together. By reporting on 116 Dwarf Syndromes (and when I started researching there were only 9 known in the world), a surgical explosion occurred on the subject, with better treatment for all Dwarfs around the world.

Eventually, I discovered the chief had told chiefs all over the USA some type of faulty information about my stay at Hopkins and it was brought up at a California teaching hospital where I had been invited to speak. Note the Network for destruction of one's good reputation that is totally undeserved. Yet, my discoveries were immediately claimed by others. As a result of all the credit being given to others, this meant that I was essentially ignored. This hurt me because of its unfairness until I realized my overriding objective had been accomplished. That objective was that, as a physician, I wanted to help people and people were helped even though I was not given credit. This was the expanding of my Consciousness on what constitutes Unconditional Love. It also opened up concepts for philosophically handling injustices occurring to me in the form of people taking credit for my work and making money from them. Such has happened all of my adult life. This way of viewing the unbalanced Scale of Personal Justice is what I call the method of Philosophical Coping. This "Seed" idea was contributed to by Mother repeatedly saying: "Son, everything happens for the best." Such came in handy for countless similar devastating things. Still, I remain on friendly terms with the predators.

Prominent in this regard has been attempts to help struggling people. They, along with almost everybody else, are not interested in the Self-Improvement help I am qualified to give. Because of their minds having been turned "Inside-Out," manifesting as self-neglect, their status quo lives are situated in not knowing what to do. They attack what goes against their Delusions of not believing what is real and believing what is not real. Furthermore, historically, Black Americans have lacked the training or exposure to role models to be any other way. This means I pay a heavy price to be of Selfless Service — and that is my definition of manifesting Unconditional Love. These lessons have taught me the hard way of how to solve or satisfactorily deal with "impossible" problems. But oddly, this pattern of Life Living leads Isolated Individualists into novel areas and working out the associated problems leads to Contentment and to the acquiring of money without ever seeking it. This invites those too lazy to work and who want to be given to, which can never be enough. Their envy, from feeling inferior, leads them to attack the Giver and thus react by being Bullies. The untold damage, seemingly too overwhelming to deal with, can only be handled by Philosophical Coping.

Once I had gotten settled in my Orthopaedic Surgery, Orthopaedic Genetics (from having taken a fellowship at Johns Hopkins in Baltimore, Maryland), and Orthopaedic Medicine (because of an intense interest in trying to keep patients from having needless surgeries), a strong Ancient African Bible message is to emphasize things of Worth (e.g., the Spiritual Beauty) over things of Value (i.e., the Material "Scarce Desires"). But since both are important, both must support each other, with Worth orchestrating. To show how this worked for me, as a reflection of my compassion, I always pursued what seemed to be of top importance — starting with where the greatest problem would lie. It did not matter that nothing was known about it — or nobody had ever been able to figure out a solution — or that no money, fame, or status would be forthcoming — or that anybody would ever know about it. If it was deemed to be the right thing to do, it did not matter what the consequences were since I knew I possessed the ingredients and enough creativity to handle anything. Examples of such situations continually occur in my life in trying to do what I can to help the truly needy people. First, it concerned dealing with those aspects of Orthopaedic Surgery no one else would undertake because of its extreme difficulty and with no financial rewards or recognition. One was Traction-Suspension for bedridden patients with bad fracture. Yet, I did not feel well trained enough to take my boards.

> "I HAD TO LEARN TO OPERATE ACCURATELY AND FAST SINCE SOME PATIENTS WERE JEHOVAH'S WITNESSES AND DID NOT ACCEPT BLOOD TRANSFUSIONS."

UNIVERSITY OF CONNECTICUT: A Black Orthopaedic Surgeon, Dick Worrell, somehow found out about me and asked me to join him as an assistant professor in Orthopaedic Surgery at the University of Connecticut, to be chief of Newington's Veterans Hospital, and to be the team physician for the Sports Department. I considered this a good opportunity to study for boards in an academic institution. It was during this time that I put my Dwarfism book together. I would sit at my desk having no idea what to say and, at times, the postman would ring the doorbell to deliver a package from different places in the world. Amazingly, a given case would correspond to what I needed to write. This is an example of the countless "Helping Hands" I continued to get. I believe this was due to my being in the Spiritual Elements flow out of which my Spiritual Entourage draws what is needed to help. Nevertheless, my separating Dwarf Syndromes into 116 types enabled the world to increase the number to the 380 presently known types. Though I never expected to make a penny for my time, energy, and effort, knowledge gained from this study is what allowed me to survive in my Orthopaedic Surgical practice and thrive (e.g., to make money). During the New Year's Rose Bowl parade, I was called out to go to the Emergency room 20 miles away from my home in Simsbury, Connecticut. So, I had to dig my car out of the snow and at that point said: "Why am I not in Los Angeles now?"

Meanwhile, I had done cryotherapy for chronic Osteoarthritis with early good results. I had also invented a surgical operation to correct clubfoot deformities that had resulted from patients who had suffered strokes. After writing up the good results of this procedure, I submitted it to the *Journal of Bone and Joint Surgery* — the top one in the world. It was rejected because there was only a 22 month follow up (monitoring of a patient's health after treatment) and their requirement was 24 months. But the chief editor told me it was very clever. Then, 9 months later that same procedure was published by a well-known institution and it quickly became a standard worldwide. This was a painful learning experience — and such was ongoing throughout my training. I learned a great deal about how youth think and what they will do and not do by being the team physician. In short, they do not believe rules apply to them.

NEWINGTON VETERANS HOSPITAL (CONNECTICUT):
There, I got a chance to deal with all types of war injuries that were and are one of a kind. This meant spending plenty of time in the anatomy lab at Yale University since I was dealing with every conceivable type of problem. I would go through textbooks that dealt with Orthopaedic problems in ancient times and supplement how they were treated then with cadaver bones and other new additions. On the case of Petock, I had to send to the Navy in Florida to get a cadaver femur to replace his tumorous one — since he did not want an Amputation. Incidentally, I sent the specimen to 10 laboratories and half said it was cancer and half said no. It was a pleasure to take a nonunion (the body's inability to heal a fracture) of the arm, repair it, and see the patient's pleasure at being able to now do things impossible prior. That was a special operation.

I had to learn to operate accurately and fast since some patients were Jehovah's Witnesses and did not accept blood transfusions. I would teach Orthopaedic Residents from Mayo Clinic, Yale, and other outstanding institutions and realized that although they had "book knowledge," they were lacking in other necessary areas. It just happened that local Orthopaedic Surgeons who had failures in treating their cases, had to transfer those failures to the VA (Veterans Affairs) Hospital. After re-operating on them and doing what I could, it was typical for them to have good results. This embarrassed many of the community Orthopaedic Surgeons and they preferred not to associate with me — even though we never had any interaction. Hostility arose there because I was younger than them and had published more papers. Thus, they did not want me to come to their conferences, and they let me know that in no uncertain terms. Yet, I needed to get the information for my boards and thus went there anyway. Then, I went to take my boards and one examiner, after he was through, offered me a job at his University. I passed the first time. Around this time, Joe Alexander, General Surgeon, invited me to join his staff at Martin Luther King/Drew Hospital in Los Angeles as Chief of Orthopaedics. I flew out "first class" — my first time — was treated well and accepted the job. After resigning from Connecticut and being under contract with King-Drew, I drove my MG into a U-Haul and packed all of my belongings around it and left for Los Angeles. When I got there, Dr. Alexander told me the community of Orthopaedic Surgeons did not want an outsider but rather one of their own to head the department. So, I got "bumped." I was told to store my belongings in their container — which I did. After finding a place to stay, I went back for my things and all were gone. I needed a job because I was "broke."

KAISER HOSPITAL IN LOS ANGELES: While at Connecticut, I had been interviewed by a recruiter from Kaiser and I re-contacted him to get a job. When I started, there was a 6-month waiting period for patients to get an appointment. I asked for and got 2 Orthopaedic technicans and 2 nurses. Within 6 weeks a patient could get an appointment the same day. The operating crew was simply outstanding. But I did not like some of Kaiser's practices in dealing with patients and decided to leave to join Dr. Compere in El Monte. I told Kaiser staff I was going to take a vacation. A month later, I got an invitation to a Kaiser party. I went and was surprised to find out it was for me — and with a lot of presents, including a radio.

EL MONTE MEDICAL CENTER: I had always wanted a convertible Cadillac since boyhood days — one of the very rare material things of interest to me. Since the Center did not pay much, I stated that renting this for me was a necessity + I needed an Orthopaedic technican. Of the several well-qualified White applicants, I passed them to take Ron Thomas, a Black guy that had absolutely no experience. So I had to do his work and mine while I farmed him out to different departments, like the operating room. Quickly, he became so outstanding that a community Orthopaedic Surgeon hired him full time. It was a pleasure operating with Dr. Compere but I did not appreciate the disrespect from the Center and decided to go into private practice.

PRIVATE ORTHOPAEDIC SURGICAL PRACTICE: Jazz was extremely important to my sanity and so was an academic institution. Hence, I chose San Bernardino but realizing the racism — and no significant decision have I ever made without considering racism — I decided to "check it out." I visited each one and to a man they said they would "welcome young blood." I took them at their word, only to realize this was a façade. When I moved there, one tried to get me to go to an "alley office" but I refused, preferring the new building at St. Bernadine's Hospital instead. They prevented me from getting on the hospital rotating staffs, a source of new patients; told community physicians not to refer patients; and had such influence as to prevent me from getting employees — as one told me, but she needed the job. I was broke and rent was due on a lot of things. I went to Long Beach where they were advertising for an Orthopaedic Surgeon but the best they could do was to refer their "Medical" — the poorest paying — to me. I went to Pasadena but the lady in charge refused to rent me office space.

So I decided to declare myself a World Authority on bony defects — an area the Industrial Arena was in need of. The local Orthopaedists thought it was immoral to take Industrial cases and so, if they took the case, it would take 9 months to get a report. But none of that made any sense to me — injured people are in need of help, regardless of how they got hurt and needed to be dealt with immediately. The situation is that if an injured worker has a bony defect in his/her back, the insurance spends millions over a lifetime on that worker. I not only promised to be able to handle such cases but I would get their reports back to them in 24 hours. That was an offer they could not refuse. When I got a case, of course, I had never seen anything like it. So, I would stay up all night going through every radiology book page by page until I found something that would give me a clue. Then I dictated it and paid a typist well to give same-day service. Also, I would go sit in the emergency room and prepare case reports, making myself available if the emergency room physician could not find any other physician to come in. It was essential for me to read all of my field because any type of case could come into the emergency room. There was no such thing as watching television or going to movies or to parties. Sleep averaged about a half hour a night. Slowly, things got easier, especially when I was appointed to be an Independent Medical Examiner for the State of California. This meant the toughest of cases were sent to me by a judge. Since millions of dollars were riding on my decisions, the attorneys were "gunning" for me. On one case, the medical records were almost as tall as me and I faltered for a moment, saying this is too much for me. Then I paused, went into my Selfhood Greatness mode, and said: "No one is better able to do this than you. They may do it differently, but no better." That was a defining moment and I never doubted myself again. The best tools I carried into my continuing life Unknowns were how to work hard and with an eagerness to immediately face and deal with any problem so as to do whatever work it took to handle it. Being in the Unknown and facing problems completely alone — and tough problems I had never seen or heard of before — required getting myself and keeping myself in order. This enabled me to know what I could count on in myself and what around me was available when encountering "alligators." The paths inside the Unknowns had/have innumerable hour-glass shaped tunnels. Within each hour-glass stricture there was a unique situation I had to figure out how to get through — a situation not allowing the use of previous solution patterns. As a result of having to observe closely every detail — learn how to arrange/rearrange and combine/recombine "bits and pieces" of facts and inferences in order to come up with creative solutions, this was a process that invariably made me stronger each time.

What was constantly reinforced was to stay focused only on the goal and proceed with a sense of urgency. There was no time to rest or do "normal" things or be involved with the Crowd since it was quite clear that the penalty for not staying "on-point" was a heavy and ongoing price that would completely stop my wholesome progress. From that moment of realization onward I had to intensify the depth of meeting problems head on and figure out ways to solve each — despite having little information, being unprepared and/or with no preconceived idea as to what to do. Of course, I made innumerable mistakes — and those mistakes would run in families as a result of having a common mentally flawed ancestor. This taught me to go to the "Seed" of the Tree type ideas of an issue and learn that "Seed" thoroughly so as to stop that chain of mistakes. In the process, I learned to see things as they are — extract teaching lessons from each mistake — and map out a plan to never allow that mistake and its family relatives to ever happen again. I never saw any reason to keep repeating the same mistake. In preparation for court, I would start my discussion from 5,000 BC as to how this type of case was handled and then progress toward the present case. This left the attorneys no place to interrupt and try to take over, based upon what they had read in Campbell's Orthopaedic text or the like. Eventually, I stopped being subpoenaed to court. I asked an attorney why and he said: "Your reports are like answers from God. The attorneys simply settle the case on what you say." It was typical for me to never be able to tell from what was in my report which side referred it. My integrity always meant more to me than making money by lying. Detail-men would come in droves and I would have to restrict them to 3 minutes. One day I asked why there were so many. He said: "You have the biggest practice in the Inland Empire."

WHAT ACHIEVEMENT "BALANCING" LOOKS LIKE: In my Orthopaedic Surgery, Orthopaedic Medicine, and Orthopaedic Genetic practice, it was usual for me to be very busy ("carefully occupied") in the true sense of the word. At one point I was seeing 120 patients a day; supervising 34 employees; actively engaged in surgery; and heavily involved with being an Agreed and Independent Medical Examiner for the state of California (that involved giving testimony in depositions and in court). A typical day included a waiting room full of patients; seemingly every employee needing help with their problems; all sorts of people (e.g., insurance companies) demanding telephone answers about patients; attorneys and a court reporter arriving in the waiting room to take my deposition; and on my part, calling to see if the operating room was ready for me to do surgery; knowing I had to get downtown to the courthouse to testify in a trial of one of my patients; seeing a host of drug detail men and women who would give me a pitch on their products (and I would limit them to three minutes); meeting with "friends" who dropped in; and squeezing in time to eat and go to the bathroom. Meanwhile, it was necessary for me to spend time with my children. Eventually, I had their playground surrounding my office at home so as to be available to them on a moment's notice and then took off every other week so as to be at home or to go on vacations. Saturdays were spent mentoring Black boys and girls. For all this to happen effectively (getting the desired results) required being extremely organized and efficient to the point of working every detail of what had to be done in order to save parts of seconds. Every reasonably successful Black American has had a great deal of experience in juggling an assortment of things in order to get things done from day to day. The key word around which Balancing for Achievement depends is Efficiency — i.e., doing things quickly and with a minimum of wasted time or energy. The degree of success depends upon one's prior Preparation skills.

During residency training, it was constant rushing from the operating room to the clinics where I might see 140 children in one morning while dictating the findings to a secretary. To flow with speed but thoroughness required a sound Philosophy of Life. To repeat, that started forming at age six when Mrs Dobbs, my AME Zion Sunday school teacher, looked at me and said: "God is Love and God is within you." This awe-inspiring concept caused Love to become the frame inside which all my choices, decisions, and solutions were made. That frame took shape from developing a work ethic — e.g., learning how to work daily at home as being part of a family unit; for pay (e.g., delivering newspapers, cutting grass, shining shoes); and for the disabled/poor/elderly for free.

I had a strong Sense of Completion — once a job was undertaken, it was essential to finish it on time. I strove to be a perfectionist (just for fun) by doing an excellent job for everything needing to be done: "If you are going to do a job, do it right."

The point was to: "Make Excellence Routine." Basic to any job was doing it with a Sense of Urgency; getting through ahead of schedule; and then helping others do their job and thus become exposed to a new set of problems that might not otherwise be available. Besides, in the process of helping others, I learned how their thoughts led to success or failure as well as learned new tools for decision-making and problem-solving. Out of this rose the practice of always keeping my word and always having an "Alternative" (i.e., other options; Plans A, B, and C). Hence, when faced with unexpected losses, lacks, or obstacles, I shifted to Plan B without losing a beat. Setbacks, failures, and people snickering at whatever I was doing spurred me to keep trying in the face of overwhelming difficulties. Creativity developed from getting around blocks people placed on my path. From hard lessons, I learned that at the completion of a job, it was important to have a place for everything, to make tools ready again, to put things back in their place, and to clean up completely.

MISSION UNDERWAY: In the mid-1970s I started on my Mission. I would collect Black youth off the streets or from the Boys and Girls Club, ranging from ages 6 to 18, take them to my office on Saturdays, and teach them how to think. My idea was that by learning how to do Critical Thinking they could diagnose and manage their own problems. But it did not work out as I had hoped. Then I realized I needed to know everything about them, starting with their (our) Ancient African Ancestors when they came on Earth 200,000 years ago. Since I had never been taught Black History, I engaged in a marathon study —

doing only that and necessities from before daybreak to bedtime, every day. But I could not find truthful or complete or in-depth Black History. Out of frustration, I cultivated an interest in words and mythology — a carryover from my Mother and inklings of its importance from studying for my Orthopaedic Surgery cases. Hence, I started researching the etymology of words but I was often dissatisfied with the findings and the meanings. Slowly, I came in contact with Ancient African knowledge of words and their meanings — an awareness so satisfying as to be like scratching the bump that itches. Thereafter, I researched meanings in both African and European literature and was continually surprised at how superficial and wrong was European information. By going through 1,000 books to find out about one word, I could establish my own meanings for a word — meanings that did not have to be revisited because the foundation was solid from knowing what everybody in the world thought about that word. I learned that somewhere inside boring works that I would rather avoid existed a jewel of Knowledge. I learned never to take shortcuts or to be lazy by limiting myself to only one reference. Also very beneficial was realizing most authorities' "dumbness"; becoming aware of their "agendas" (racism orientation like having all pictures of Ancient Egyptians modeled by White people) and bias; and their philosophy (e.g., of not believing in the metaphysical). Thus, I did not have to take what they said and build on it.

Instead, since the 1980s, I have branched off into realms involving my own novel ideas and have never used any more European information in dealing with Afrocentric topics. Once I could get a solid foundation for the meanings of words out of Ancient African literature I could then start formulating sound thought structures. These became so plentiful that I was forced to start making my own dictionary. Although I could spend up to 3 days researching one word, the meaningful results did not remain in my memory for long — and hence the need for my own dictionary. A surprising by-product was that so much time spent on one word meant that word acted like a sun with its countless rays. Hence, I could go off in many directions from that word's totipotency and that opened paths into previously unknown realms. Focusing on discerning Principles to serve as the philosophical building blocks of African Tradition and fitting these together into harmony clearly show that all real things — both Unseeable and Seeable things — are connected (the Law of Sympathy). I learned there are only a few basic principles (unchanging realities) and to know those seeds helps to understand or figure out the Tree Concept in any problem or situation of life. The next step was to focus on interrelationships of principles — particularly the inner nature of what externally seemed different.

Putting new paths of knowledge together, even though uncertain of their accuracy, allowed me months later to revise the "skeletal" concept as I gained more information. This accumulated Knowledge formed Wisdom Seeds. From those Seeds certain family related things could be inferred — like knowing what one's parents stress gives a good idea of what their children will do in later life. I discovered that although I would spend an excessive amount of time on a new concept in order to arrive at its Seed, not long thereafter, that seed could be used to explain something that had earlier seemed "impossible" to solve and on which I would have spent a great deal of time in vain. The seed would also give insight as to how to approach something new as well as give me the missing link for looking at something common in an uncommon way or seeing the uncommon in the common. For example, the work I put into trying to understand Spiritual Hope helped expand my mind and increase my awareness in multiple other areas. I always liked silly humor because it kept my mind flexible inside a fun atmosphere and offered options. It really helps to have multiple projects in various stages of development because when I learn something for one, it usually applies in several other areas. I never was stopped because a problem was too difficult — and never considered how tough something was that had to be done. Instead, for something overwhelming, I would do something or put down something and add to it over the weeks. I wanted to know every piece of information because even the weird stuff would one day be the answer for an impossible problem. I never approach a problem from using the way it has always been done. Nor do I discard out-of-date information because something can be added to it to bring it up to date. I learned that going to the trouble of discovering how people evolved was the best way to gain insight as to how they are now and why they do what they do. That helps me tolerate the bad they do that I do not like. Keeping with Manners for them and maintaining a Free Mind for me requires letting them know what they do that is not in my best interest. To this end, I use humor whenever possible — and when that works, it is a display of Wisdom. Still, I know that those most in need of philosophical help reject it the most. But since it is my Mission, I must continue doing what I can to help struggling Black youth when they are ready to receive it 50 years from now. Using the rejections I get from them serves as a path to let me know what to focus on and where and how to start.

For example, one of the first things they need to know is that being made in the Image of God means each human is a miniature universe orchestrated by the Spark of God. Thus, to understand any part of the universe is to understand all of it, including one's Selfhood having Selfhood Greatness. To recover that awareness which every human had at birth is the way to switch from one's False Self back to one's newborn Real Self. Then one starts with Common Sense things that lead to Knowledge.

Examples include: Understanding comes when one liberates oneself from the old and so makes possible a direct, unmediated contact with the new, the mystery, moment by moment, of one's existence. Call things by their right names. Know one's own follies and faults and how to correct them so as to shine within. It is fundamental early on to know how to protect oneself. Seek Good that will be forever. Cherish the greatness and power that comes from self-mastery — know what is best to know and do what is best to do — do things when living that will make you proud when you come to the end of your days. Judge by what one does with what one has. After all, true success may not be about the height one attains but about the depths from which one came. Be wiser than others by seeing things the way they are and knowing what everybody else knows — but do not tell them so. What I now know is that Knowledge and water have much in common — some descends from above; some springs from below the surface; and some flows in between. In other words, some is from Divine revelation; some is from the light of Nature; and some is within one's own Divine Consciousness. Knowledge comes by taking these things apart — properly assessing each part for its Spiritual Elements content — do the shedding, maneuvering and manipulations that lead to harmony when the remaining ingredients are meshed together for a decision or solution. Knowledge is acquired by success in fitting a new experience into the system of concepts based upon one's old experiences. Then pertinent details of knowledge are swallowed up in principles so they can be put together for making use of this Knowledge. The active utilization of Knowledge is the final possession of wisdom. Wisdom's worthwhileness and the associated happiness comes from within itself. People often ask me if I feel proud about my achievements. That always causes me to remember Smitty telling me: "You do not expect to get compliments for what you are supposed to do." What I do is what I am supposed to do in keeping with my Talent within a "ME/WE" context. I would like the information I work hard to produce to get to the struggling Black youth for whom it is intended. This would require a group of dedicated and focused Black adults with good Common Sense and on all rungs of the ladder to come together and fashion a chain designed to pull these youth out of the "bottomless pit" they are in. Those of the lower rungs can both guide us as to how to go about selecting the topic and then be the translators for delivering, for that is not one of my skills. Thus, I see myself as only one link in the chain. I have a vision of what is ultimate success for me and that is to start an expanding program of taking struggling Black Youth onto a farm to live and see them become nourished from being in Nature, to allow them to discover and develop their Talents. I forget about people telling me they have benefited from my ideas. A problem with today's youth is that they want compliments for doing a sloppy partial job.

I have never understood why people are so dependent on the Crowd. Perhaps they are so insecure as to need compliments as a measure of where they are in relation to the Crowd. My standard is how well I have done a necessary job, as a measure of self-pride. I cannot expect compliments from others because we think differently and have different goals. What I do requires hard work, time, and energy — and people are not willing to work that hard). Thus, I move on because I can move faster alone. Yet, I truly enjoy a few good friends. I do not know any other way to be other than who I am. Neither will I allow people to be abusive without letting them know. I simply avoid them. Also, I now realize, after countless painful lessons, that I cannot help the masses, for their "Don't Care" clinging position is clear. I work to share with those like-minded people who desire to improve with my help.

Notes & Reflections

> "WE SPEND THE FIRST YEAR OF A CHILD'S LIFE TEACHING IT TO WALK AND TALK AND THE REST OF ITS LIFE TO SHUT UP AND SIT DOWN. THERE'S SOMETHING WRONG THERE."
>
> - NEIL DEGRASSE TYSON

34

Dr. Bill Guillory

100% Personal Responsibility

CHAPTER THIRTY-FOUR

Dr. Bill Guillory

President/CEO - Innovations International, Inc. Salt Lake City, Utah, USA

Dr. William A. Guillory is one of the most dynamic transformational speakers, and conference and seminar facilitators. He speaks about subjects that are at the forefront of our thinking, such as Creating Virtually Inclusive Workspaces; The FuturePerfect Organization — Driven by Quantum-Thinking; The Confluence of Human Potential and Technology Integration; Creating a Culture of Compatibility; Diversity – The Unifying Force of the 21st Century; and Higher-Order Creativity and Consciousness Exploration.

Personal and Professional Success

"If you are participating in an activity driven by your passion, your personal and professional success are One - inseparable."

> "WHEN I ASSIST OTHERS IN TERMS OF PERSONAL TRANSFORMATION, IT IS NOT BECAUSE I AM HELPING THEM, BUT BECAUSE THEY SERVE AS VEHICLES FOR MY PERSONAL LEARNING AND GROWTH OF HOW TO BECOME A HUMAN BEING. THEY SHOULD BE ACKNOWLEDGED AND REWARDED, NOT ME!"

I define success as living true to my passion in practically all of my life activities — regardless of the outcome. What counts is not selling out and falling short of my capability.

The foundation of my success is based upon 100% personal responsibility, as a predisposed mind-set, and accepting 100% personal accountability for the results I produce — sometimes in concert with others. This foundation allows me the freedom to create my own reality and leads to the quote below:

"If you can master personal responsibility,
you can master the human experience."

My personal passion is to influence the inhabitants of planet Earth to experience transformation from a survival mentality to compatibility — compassion, caring, and contribution to the health, happiness, and well-being of others.

The various forms (expressions) my passion has taken are: university professor conducting research in chemical physics; human resource consultant/facilitator in diversity, high performance, and quantum-thinking; public speaker and writer facilitating human transformation; and writer of books, white papers, and videos freely distributed to the public (https://thewayoftheheart.org) for reflection, learning, and personal transformation.

Other attributes, such as commitment, and personal and spiritual growth (channeling), are examples of living consistent with empowerment, integrity, and commitment to the success and well-being of others — from which I naturally derive my greatest personal success.

Other expressions include: The Center for Creativity and Inquiry (Think Tank for Innovations); Innovations International, Inc. (Consulting Influence on Corporations and Organizations, Globally); The Way of the Heart Website (Influence the Global Consciousness to Transform from Survival to Compatibility) as conduits for my life's activities.

"When I assist others in terms of personal transformation, it is not because I am helping them, but because they serve as vehicles for my personal learning and growth of how to become a human being. They should be acknowledged and rewarded, not me!"

Notes & Reflections

> "YOU SHOULD TREAT FAME LIKE A RENTAL CAR. TAKE A SPIN AROUND THE BLOCK. THAT WAY WHEN THEY TAKE THE CAR BACK, YOU WON'T FEEL LIKE THEY'RE TAKING A PIECE OF YOU."
>
> **- TREVOR NOAH**

35

Kristen L. Pope

The World, Needs YOU!

CHAPTER THIRTY-FIVE

Kristen L. Pope

Speaker, Host, CEO and Founder of Pope Productions, Inc.

Kristen L. Pope, the multi-hyphenate visionary, is also the creator of the On Air Academy which aims at increasing representation in TV news and reframing the narrative about communities of color with balanced storytelling. The award-winning TV journalist and multi-media strategist manages social media at Harvard University in the Division of Continuing Education.

What Do You Believe?

When you look at a person's life, and observe their actions, you will understand what they believe in. Success has everything to do with what you believe. If you believe you are successful or can be successful, you will be. Keep in mind, success is subjective. It's based on your belief system: not a dollar amount, or a status level, or a ring on the fourth finger

> "THE GREAT THING ABOUT HABITS IS THAT WE CAN CHANGE THEM. THE GREAT THING ABOUT BELIEF IS THAT WE CAN CHANGE IT. IF THERE IS A NEED TO ADJUST, YOU CAN, AND YOU SHOULD TO THE DEGREE THAT YOU DON'T LOSE YOURSELF BUT INSTEAD DISCOVER THE NEXT AND BEST LEVEL OF YOURSELF."

of your left hand. You'll never believe you are successful measuring your achievements against someone else's. The first step to success is anchoring yourself in the core tenet that you are worthy. In his speech, "What is Your Life's Blueprint?" Reverend Dr. Martin Luther King said, "Number one in your life's blueprint should be: a deep belief in your own dignity, your own worth and your own somebodiness. Don't allow anybody to make you feel that you are nobody. Always feel that you count. Always feel that you have worth, and always feel that your life has ultimate significance." This is the beginning of all success. You have to believe you are worthy to become your version of success.

You may ask, am I not successful, because I don't yet see what I believe? The answer is that's up to you. Success is not a singular event. Success happens along the journey. Don't spend your journey waiting and working towards moments, only. Enjoy those moments because there is often where you realize how successful you really are.

I have had times in my life when it seemed that my family was successful, but my career was mediocre, or my career was thriving but family was starving. I have found that, for me, success looks like two distinct aspects: the first, alignment with my highest belief for myself. This alignment includes fulfilling the purpose for my life and why I was created; alignment with my values, personal life mission, my professional mission, my family mission, my financial goals and mission, our emotional, spiritual, and mental state. The second, impact. When my life impacts another life positively and helps push a person to where they want or need to go, I am successful in the mission and purpose I was sent to accomplish.

The qualities that have helped me arrive here include: authenticity, wisdom, surrender, vulnerability, being a visionary, taking risks, expecting more from myself, working hard and smart, surrounding myself with people smarter than myself, love, service and belief in a mission greater than myself. The character traits that have served me well are resilience, tenacity, flexibility, ability to connect with people, being a community builder, forgiveness, loyalty, kindness, integrity, humor, charisma and persistent faith.

In addition to our belief are our habits that determine our success. We are our habits. The positive ones and the ones that work against us. Some of the habits that have served me well include:

- Practicing my faith as a lifestyle. My faith is not event based, it's a lifestyle
- Prayer
- Studying the bible's scriptures
- Studying Jesus Christ's life
- Seeking out wisdom and wise counsel
- Being prepared for the opportunity I want to come my way
- Commitment to excellence
- Getting back up after I fail or learn a lesson

The last habit has helped me to survive this life and press on to success when it seemed out of reach. The great thing about habits is that we can change them. The great thing about belief is that we can change it. If there is a need to adjust, you can, and you should to the degree that you don't lose yourself but instead discover the next and best level of yourself.

I intend to take all of these traits, habits, and beliefs with me into my next endeavors as a businesswoman, media coach, speaker, storyteller, philanthropist, mother, wife, community leader, disciple of Jesus Christ, daughter and friend.

As you seek out success, keep in mind, the ingredients are not external, they're internal and so is its greatest manifestation: the intangible fruit it produces like peace, joy, kindness, and love.

You define success for yourself and stick to it in spite of what society tries to sell you. Hold fast to your belief, your values and best of all, the characteristics that make you, you. The world doesn't need a _____. Fill in the blank. The world, needs you. And when the world experiences the full expression of your best you, impact and success are inevitable.

Notes & Reflections

> "DO NOT CALL FOR BLACK POWER OR GREEN POWER. CALL FOR BRAIN POWER."

— BARBARA JORDAN

36

Jeremy Cutts

I'm Built For Struggle

CHAPTER THIRTY-SIX

Jeremy Cutts, AIA

Architectural Associate, Williams Blackstock Architects, Auburn, AL

In 2021, Jeremy Cutts won the AIA (American Institute of Architects) Alabama Young Architects Award, which "recognizes individuals who have demonstrated exceptional leadership and made significant contributions to the architecture profession early in their careers." Jeremy attended Auburn University between 2005 and 2010 and graduated with a Bachelor of Architecture (B. Arch.) degree.

Childhood Environment and Family Background

I credit a lot of who I am to my family dynamic and how I grew up. My parents were not together; I lived with my mother and spent summers with my father, so I grew up between two worlds.

> "MY DEFINITION OF SUCCESS CONTINUES TO EVOLVE, BUT THE ROOT OF IT IS "TO HELP OTHERS REACH THEIR FULL POTENTIAL, WHILE MAINTAINING THE LIFESTYLE THAT I WANT FOR MY FAMILY.""

My father was an army brat, born in Germany; he lived in many places before his parents settled in Huntsville, Alabama when he was a teenager. His father eventually retired from the military and later from the postal service. His mother (an immigrant from Jamaica) eventually obtained a college degree and went on to retire from a career in government defense contracting. They were a comfortably middle-class family.

My mother was born and raised in Alabama, with goals of doing and seeing more. Her parents and grandparents were Alabama natives; the family owned land in the countryside, near Huntsville. My mother's parents moved to Huntsville, where her father worked for industrial companies and her mother worked in healthcare. Both of my mother's parents were stricken with health conditions which left them on disability, unable to work. For them, financial stability always seemed just out of reach, but they exemplified the idea that the people you love and those who love you can make life as rich as any amount of money.

Seventy-five percent of each year, I spent with my mother's family, in one reality, which gave me determination: I'm built for struggle; I know how bad things can be; and most importantly, I know I can handle things, no matter how bad they get.

Twenty-five percent of each year, I spent with my father's family, in a different reality, which gave me vision: I was exposed to and understood that there was more in the world than what I saw in my main reality; I knew it was possible to achieve more.

Early Influences and Tendencies

I am influenced constantly, but I choose what to keep and what to let go. I learned early on that there are people in life from whom you can learn what to do, and there are people in life from whom you can learn what not to do...both are equally important influences.

I am the eldest grandchild on both sides of my family, and as such, I was the first to make many of the mistakes that children make. As a child, I never wanted to disappoint my elders; I wanted to make them proud. As I got older, I had to set an example for my younger siblings, cousins, and friends; I never wanted to let them down; I wanted to make them proud. As a husband and a father, I never want to let my family down; I want to make them proud. That being said, I am not one to regret things in life. I truly believe that everything happens for a reason and things work out the way that they are supposed to work out.

Challenges Faced; Opportunities Taken in Adolescence

Life is filled with challenges, great and small. When faced with any challenge/obstacle, I tend to focus on "doing what I can with what I've got."

As an elementary school student, I had the opportunity to be a recess-buddy with a child in my grade who had special needs. Periodically throughout the school year, I would spend my recess with this child; learning how to interact effectively; understanding his capabilities; and realizing how much we had in common. I believe that experience strengthened my sense of empathy and my ability to view things from a different perspective. Bob Marley has a song lyric which goes "Every man thinks that his burden is the heaviest..." I realize that challenges are all relative.

Experience in the Business World

I feel that my life experience is different from many of my colleagues in this profession and they have prepared me in ways that are unique amongst my peers. Because of this, I think that I provide insight, perspective, and sometimes a voice that is refreshing, or at least thought-provoking. However, I often feel like other people are somehow better prepared for the business world than I was; as though they have this "game" figured out – what this is all about and how to navigate it – while I'm slowly picking up on the rules and the object of this "game"; realizing what skills are best suited and how I can use what I've got to do what I can to survive, if not thrive.

Definition of Success

My definition of success continues to evolve, but the root of it is "to help others reach their full potential, while maintaining the lifestyle that I want for my family."

Advice for Young People

Young People: be yourself, as authentically as you know how. The people, things, and opportunities that are for you, will present themselves. Recognize that you don't achieve anything great in life without help; be thankful and grateful to all who have aided you. Do what you can with what you've got.

Notes & Reflections

> " I AM DRIVEN BY TWO MAIN PHILOSOPHIES: KNOW MORE TODAY ABOUT THE WORLD THAN I KNEW YESTERDAY AND LESSEN THE SUFFERING OF OTHERS. YOU'D BE SURPRISED HOW FAR THAT GETS YOU. "

- DR. NEIL DEGRASSE TYSON

37

Dr. William A. Lester, Jr.

Hold Fast To Dreams

CHAPTER THIRTY-SEVEN

Professor William A. Lester, Jr.

Professor Emeritus, Chemistry, University of California, Berkeley

In honor of Professor's Lester's distinguished service as an educator, the College of Chemistry at UC, Berkeley, has established a lectureship named for him. As the Dean of the College, Douglas Clark noted, "Bill Lester is a great scientist and wonderful colleague who has made important contributions to the College and our profession on many levels, including his tireless efforts to promote diversity within chemical education and professional practice. He is an exemplary role model, and I cannot imagine a better way to recognize his legacy."

YOU are responsible for your career

I have a message for young people borne out of my experiences that I want to share. It is that you are responsible for your career. Advice from others can

> "HOLD FAST TO DREAMS, FOR IF DREAMS DIE, LIFE IS A BROKEN WINGED BIRD THAT CANNOT FLY."
>
> - LANGSTON HUGHES

be useful and is to be understood and appreciated, but you must make the final judgments in light of what you want to do, and your objective determination of your abilities.

Be willing to work hard and do those things that are positive. Be open to new points of view and methods of achieving your basic goals.

Further, a point my father made to me during my senior year of high school I found invaluable, "you can do anything in life you put your mind to."

Finally, I leave you with the words of Langston Hughes that have been important to my family, and I hope may be of some benefit to you, "Hold fast to dreams, for if dreams die, life is a broken winged bird that cannot fly."

~~~

Professor William Lester is a distinguished theoretical chemist and UC Berkeley professor. He attended all-Black elementary schools in Chicago, Illinois due to racial segregation. After World War II, Professor Lester's family moved to a new neighborhood where he had the chance to attend a formerly all-White high school. He later earned a B.S degree in 1958 and an M.S. in chemistry in 1959 from the University of Chicago. In 1964, he obtained his Ph.D. in chemistry from the Catholic University of America, Washington, D.C.

While on a postdoctoral appointment at the University of Wisconsin, Madison, Professor Lester worked on the molecular collision theory and later at IBM Corporation, San Jose, California, he served as the director of the National Resource for Computation in Chemistry and led the first unified effort in computational chemistry in the United States. His research efforts at Berkeley extended the powerful quantum Monte Carlo method into a wider range of chemical problems. He has published over 200 papers in his field, won numerous research and teaching awards, and served on the editorial boards of the *Journal of Physical Chemistry, International Journal of Quantum Chemistry, Journal of Computational Chemistry, Computer Physics Communications,* and the *Journal of Chemical Physics.* He was also elected a fellow of the American Physical Society, the American Chemical Society, and the American Association for the Advancement of Science.

Notes & Reflections

> "AT YOUR HIGHEST MOMENT, BE CAREFUL. THAT'S WHEN THE DEVIL COMES FOR YOU."
>
> - DENZEL WASHINGTON

38

George in Florence, Italy

George Hofstetter

Trust, Cultivation, &

Inner Curiosity

CHAPTER THIRTY-EIGHT

George Hofstetter

CEO, Founder, Software Engineer

At the age of 16, George pioneered GHTech Inc., in hopes of helping other New Afrikan(Black) and Brown students and adults gain entry into the world of technology as innovators, and to change the world's perspective on race through technology.

Trust

There are three major tools, skills and methodologies that have helped me stay on a positive trajectory through consistency, motivation, grounding, and confidence along my journey. The first skill is TRUST. I trust myself and my inner genius. I encourage people to "trust yourself and your inner genius."

Growing up in the United States educational system as a New Afrikan(Black person), or a person of color, we

> "DR. ANGELA Y. DAVIS ONCE TOLD ME TO PRACTICE HOLDING SPACE FOR WHAT WE CANNOT YET CONCEPTUALIZE."

are systemically minimized, discriminated against and criminalized for just "being" in education. It's extremely challenging to believe in our genius or intelligence when the classrooms, educators, and curricula we are learning from are systematically, and intentionally designed to oppress, not only our creativity but our ability to truly learn. The educational system of the United States is designed to strip away our self-confidence, dismantle the fundamentals of critical thinking, and further encourage damaging rhetoric for communities of color to create a class of intellectually and economically dependent workers. That's why the first skill to practice is to believe in yourself, your value, and to begin to trust your genius that has been buried inside you, longing to self express.

Cultivation

The second skill is CULTIVATION. It's critically important to cultivate a network of support. This means building our village that we will have to turn to when we need guidance, community, and collaboration. A phrase that has stuck with me is, "If you want to go fast, go alone; if you want to go far, go together." It's true. When we are at our lowest, in between a rock and a hard place, we need to be able to turn to our community (whether it be two people or twenty-two people) for support and grounding. When everything begins to feel overwhelming, it's a wonderful reminder that we are never truly alone.

Innate Curiosity

The last skill is one of my favorites; I call it a superpower. Our INNATE CURIOSITY. As part of growing into my adulthood, I've seen how systems and institutions diminish people's curiosity. The myth of 'asking a stupid question,' is just that, a myth. The mantra for Virgil Abloh, who was the Lead Creative Director for Louis Vuitton and founder of the Off-white luxury brands, was "Question everything!"

George in Paris, France

From early on in primary school when we are our truest selves, we question everything all the time because the correlation of curiosity and fear that is reinforced by social perception is not fully developed yet. The curiosity has not been 'schooled' out of us yet. Fostering our innate curiosity is what I believe we all need to get back to, what we need to routinely practice everyday. A healthy curiosity feeds a healthy mind. Dr. Angela Y. Davis once told me to practice holding space for what we cannot yet conceptualize. I believe that's only possible through living a life of positive curiosity.

I believe that a world without the influence of white supremacy, neo colonialism and imperialistic behaviors is possible. I believe it's possible through community, connection, and curiosity. Curiosity to seek solutions to help others, not just ourselves. I encourage you to follow these three methodologies and join me on this journey of success through trust, cultivation and curiosity.

~~~

Since the age of 13 George has developed various projects from iOS app store approved mobile applications, to web-platforms, and has lectured at multiple universities and educational institutions, as well as corporations, both domestically and across the world.

Some of George's projects include the following:

- The creation and launch of a social networking app designed for education for a California based non-profit called Kingmakers of Oakland
- Being featured in the documentary, Use of Force: The policing of Black America (co-produced by Chuck D from Public Enemy)
- Teaching and developing the (in)Visible Designers series at Stanford University's d.school (Hasso Plattner Institute of Design)
- Building Up to Code Academy Vol. 1, a free online computer science and entrepreneurship curriculum sponsored by Capital One Dev Exchange
- Sharing his thoughts in his TEDx Talk at the Seattle Academy of Arts and Sciences

Notes & Reflections

> "I AM URGING THAT WE SHOULD LEARN ABOUT PEOPLE IN OTHER PLACES, TAKE AN INTEREST IN THEIR CIVILIZATIONS, THEIR ARGUMENTS, THEIR ERRORS, THEIR ACHIEVEMENTS NOT BECAUSE THAT WILL BRING US TO AGREEMENT, BUT BECAUSE IT WILL HELP US GET USED TO ONE ANOTHER."

- DR. KWAME ANTHONY APPIAH

39

Dr. Ivory V. Nelson

Education Must Glory in the Privilege of Doubt

CHAPTER THIRTY-NINE

Dr. Ivory V. (Vance) Nelson

President Emeritus, Lincoln University

Dr. Nelson served as the first Black chancellor of Alamo Community College District in San Antonio (1986-1992), the first Black president of Central Washington University in Ellensburg, Washington (1992-1999) and president of Lincoln University (1999-2012). Dr. Nelson's vast experience in education and leadership are encapsulated in the following excerpts from some of his writings and speeches.

On Education: Glory in the Privilege of Doubt

Education in a contemporary society is not an activity confined within the walls of the familiar institutions of teaching and learning; rather, it is a pervasive molding force that affects all individuals in our society, intellectually, creatively, and economically.

> "YOUNG PEOPLE SHOULD BE EDUCATED TO VALUE INDIVIDUALITY AND CREATIVITY ABOVE CONFORMITY AND PACKAGED OPINIONS."

Education must provide a system that is sensitive to social needs and pursue quality without compromise. Education should be accessible, diverse, and flexible; it should allow for transfer among institutions and among programs; it should be equitable in its treatment of all without regard to economic status, race, creed, color, sex, or national origin.

Education must perform useful social functions that will ensure the socialization of the young, provide for the transmission of a cultural heritage, provide the trained manpower for the corporate establishment, provide certification for entry into the professions, provide a means for upward social mobility, and provide a sanctuary for scholars and artists.

Education must be accountable to the public for the proper deliverance of societal needs by ensuring that educational programs:

1. communicate with all parties;
2. have an organized philosophy or plan of action that has the allegiance of everyone;
3. are based on ethical principles and policies that work;
4. are specific about their purpose;
5. improve the performance of all persons involved;
6. are sensitive to human needs;
7. have all persons touched by the program participate in its development from start to finish; and
8. provide easy access for all groups.

Education has to be nurtured, and kept alive and healthy, not merely permitted to exist for the sake of utilitarian gains when particular types of solutions are needed for crisis or crash endeavors.

Education for the masses has to be conceptualized as a national system, which is indispensable to the workings of a democratic society. Education must be a concept that is broadly understood and accepted. The national commitment to education has to be so compelling that it cannot be circumvented through a variety of subterfuges and overridden by a reshuffling of national priorities.

The educational enterprise must establish goals of efficiency, expediency, power, status, and success. Young people should be educated to value individuality and creativity above conformity and packaged opinions. Participants in the educational process shall utilize tools to evince concern, commitment, and social sensitivity to their fellow human beings above personal acceptance and mere social success.

Education must glory in the privilege of doubt. Intellectual progress is made by finding fault with the best thought presented. Agreement must be designed for the privilege of learning, not for the therapy of dogmatic assertion. Serenity is sought in the exhaustion of reason rather than by turning off the hearing aid.

Education must give its priority to the significant bond of men and women who believe that the worth or dignity of knowledge does not depend solely upon its current usefulness. In education, we must realize that man's wisdom and understanding are ends in themselves.

Education must ensure that every individual has a right to success and that society has a stake in everybody's participation. All interests must be served individually and collectively.

On Defining Leadership

What comes to your mind when you hear the word leadership? Do you think of international figures like Martin Luther King, Jr., Nelson Mandela, Bill Gates, Bob Johnson and General Colin Powell?

Our brains somehow immediately translate the word leadership to mean leader. You probably just did the same thing. If asked for a definition of leadership, I would define leadership as a rational process of getting people working together to accomplish change or to make a difference that will benefit the common good. Robert P. Luciano would say, "leaders cajole, inspire and yes, coerce people to do something, to take action toward a goal." And that is what I want young potential leaders to do. Commit yourselves to cajoling, inspiring, and yes, coercing people to do something, to take action toward a common goal.

In order to develop the skill level to accomplish goals, there are at least ten certain characteristics that can be considered key and necessary for leaders. These characteristics must become a part of your muscle memory. Additionally, you must constantly engage in a program of self-development to acquire these skills and attitudes that are characteristic of a successful leader. At the heart of that self-development, there must be a willingness to lead, a capability for taking care of details, a firmness in holding on to higher goals, an ability to marshal successfully one's own energies and an ability to make the most of the work of others.

Let me now provide a description and an understanding of the ten characteristics of leaders.

> "A TYPICAL QUESTION BY A POTENTIAL LEADER IN ANY BAD SITUATION IS TO ASK: 'WHERE DID I GO WRONG?' YOU SHOULD DO THIS PRIOR TO ANY ATTEMPT TO ASSESS FAULT OR BLAME SOMEONE ELSE."

1. The ability to communicate a vision for the future

Generally, the opportunity to think in big terms and to develop a vision is often resisted because of the nagging obligations of thinking small. The successful leader of the 21st Century will have a vision that provides for the freeing of the mind and the creation of a process for the cultivation of the habit of thinking about what your true goals really are. The ability to look ahead is not just a matter of curiosity — it is a matter of adaptation. Hegel, a noted philosopher, once wrote: "Hell is truth seen too late." The visionary looking ahead is practicing leadership by trying to seize hold of the future and to guide it, not just react to what otherwise will happen.

2. Understanding and caring for human beings

The recognition that people come first and the wise treatment of human beings is a fundamental necessity for understanding and caring. The application of leadership development lies in the ability of the leader to bring and use those qualities of personality and character essential to the complex task of bringing out the best in others. Thus, it is essential that a leader must develop the art of giving support, encouragement and reinforcement to others, and be that invisible person, who steps forward, supporting and motivating others in time of need and crisis. The leader who assists others to know and find genuine pleasure in performance of their jobs will provide incentive and comfort in obtaining quality performance. It goes without saying that a leader must exhibit happiness and joy in his work. J Kami in 1972, writes that "leading by fear and leading by enthusiasm are two ways of leading." However, leading by enthusiasm gets the job done.

3. The ability to develop and cultivate a monitoring and mentoring network

Successful leaders can point to someone who has served as their mentor. Mentoring allows the potential leader to learn and apply new skills in new contexts and to exercise new responsibilities associated with whatever type of leadership role the individual pursues. Generally, mentoring assignments allow the opportunity for the intern to experience a variety of leadership and management styles. Additionally, the mentee can interact with new constituencies and develop different perspectives on a particular organization. It has long been conventional wisdom that the best way to learn a subject is to have firsthand experience. A good mentoring program can lead to successful networking.

4. Understand risk-taking and know when, where, and how much risk you should take for any given idea or proposal

Never risk more than you can afford to lose. Subjective confusion is in the nature of the word "risk" itself. You must strongly consider the question of whether "telling it like it is" is riskier or less risky than keeping your mouth shut in a crucial situation. You ought to determine how much there is to lose either way. If you are open in a highly volatile situation, chances are that you will be severely reprimanded, distrusted or even fired. You must be aware that saying nothing may be seen as weaseling, weak, and that you are not capable of greater responsibility. You must carefully weigh the values of your peers, supervisors, social norms and where you, as a leader, want your career to go. Only after this assessment should you make a decision on the route to take. You should be careful not to risk the future by not taking any risks in the present. An inflexible value system, a reflexive approach to problem solving, and a consistently cautious manner generally gives the impression that the decision-making process is based on immediate security rather than immediate facts. You must remember there is a difference between taking a chance when there is no control over the odds and taking risks in a situation where the incumbent is a factor with some weight. Prudent advice suggests that you should view each situation on its own merits by not letting past history or the fear of risk stifle the intuitive decision-making process. The person who cannot take risks, expose their ignorance, and chart a true sense of direction will fall short in achieving any leadership position.

5. Learning from adversity and accepting responsibility

One of the most difficult problems is the development of an attitude that allows one to make use of adverse situations and accept responsibility for the problem one finds. A typical question by a potential leader in any bad situation is to ask. "Where did I go wrong?" You should do this prior to any attempt to assess fault or blame someone else. It is difficult for one who intends or portends to be a leader unless there is recognition that adversity and responsibility are assets and not liabilities. When was the last time someone was recruited to a leadership position and that position did not carry a good deal of adversarial elements. Remember, usually one is not needed if the situation is functioning properly. Having the capability to profit from adverse situations will generally advance one's career faster than many other items. In other words, if one can be viewed as that individual who can function under pressure, fire, criticism, and attack, generally that individual is viewed as good leadership material.

6. Always exhibit a high degree of optimism

The leader who views the glass as half-full rather than as half-empty sends the message that situations can be handled positively rather than negatively. If you are seeking a leadership position you should not give off signals such as pomposity, false modesty, indecisiveness, evasion, narrowness of vision, insecurity, secretiveness, remoteness and aloofness; these are bad signs. Prospective leaders must show a high degree of optimism without showing an overbearing strength of personality or conviction. Generally, candidates will eliminate themselves from potential leadership positions, if their optimism does not provide some degree of safety. How to match the positive traits and show great imagination, ideas and conviction, without diminishing one's optimism is necessary for any potential leader to obtain a leadership role.

7. A fervent desire for excellence

It is not credible to talk of becoming a successful leader without expressing a very strong commitment to high standards and excellence in whatever endeavor you wish to pursue. In expressing the need to design systems that aid and assist the disadvantaged, you must be careful not to create the impression that you are lowering standards. Respecting high standards and excellence, yet recognizing the imperfections that exist, bodes well for any successful leader.

8. Take the long view against expedient solutions to problems of the moment and expedient solutions to career goals and aspirations

The need for instant gratification in a career will stifle the opportunity for a prospective leader to succeed in his/her career goals and aspirations. Opportunities come at the most inopportune times. Thus, one must be prepared to take advantage the moment that opportunity presents itself. The willingness to consider moving to out-of-the-way places, the entertainment of talk of receiving less salary, and the willingness to take on impossible situations are key ingredients in taking the long view. It is often asked when someone should begin looking for the next

> "SUCCESS IN ANY CAREER DEPENDS HEAVILY ON THE ABILITY TO TAKE RAW DATA AND FASHION A SOLUTION TO THE PROBLEM AT HAND THAT MAKES THE PEOPLE AFFECTED FEEL A PART OF THE ANSWER."

opportunity. You must be ready to take detours, side roads, and alleyways to obtain experience, power, and visibility. The Yellow Brick Road, for most persons, is usually dirt and grit, not gold. Taking the long view for expedient solutions for successfully solving problems or resolving conflict usually prevents quick irrational decision-making. You must carefully assess whether the problem resolution is good for the moment or that the solution will stand the test of time and high scrutiny. You must remember that a leader, especially if they are a minority, is more visible in many respects than their counterparts. Every action or inaction will suffer the review of stiffer requirements than their counterpart. There is an old axiom, if it does not play well tomorrow, chances are you should not do it today.

9. In higher education, a successful leader must have strong academic credentials

This ninth requirement for a successful leader is a tricky one. Upon examining the patterns for selecting leaders in higher education (especially minorities), it becomes clear that the doctorate degree is the passport to the leadership chair. Institutions of higher education and faculty generally look for the doctorate for its leadership positions. Minorities who aspire to leadership roles in higher education should remember that while leadership positions advertised sometimes will carry the statement that less than the doctorate is required, the doctorate is preferred; they will generally waste their time participating in the application process, unless there is some inside connection within the organization for which the leadership position is sought.

10. The ability to have a liberated mind
Higher order thinking skills mixed with recognition of the needs of people are good indicators of professional competence. It is worth noting here that most issues are not black and white and are not clear-cut. The pure use of statistical data and absolute facts without knowledge and wisdom of the people or the organizational environment is a sure way to become an ineffective leader. Success in any career depends heavily on the ability to take raw data and fashion a solution to the problem at hand that makes the people affected feel a part of the answer. Too many leaders make the cardinal mistake of assuming that the facts speak for themselves and that any decision is dictated by how the facts are arrayed and presented. A liberated mind usually requires the ability to ask the pertinent questions, "Why are you doing it this way? Are there newer and better ways to accomplish the goal? Are we simply doing this because it is the usual way?" While facts, figures and information may suggest the recommended approach, good wisdom and knowledge about the total picture will help form the solution by taking into consideration the human element and the environmental concerns of the organization.

Much of what I have presented here are thoughts and reflections on how these characteristics have affected my career. They are presented as guideposts and ideas for reflection and thinking. It is my honest opinion that if you use these characteristics as a guidepost, success, while not guaranteed, will come a lot easier.

On Risk Taking
Dr. Samuel Massie, a Black Educator, used to give an inspiring speech to young Black children in the South. It was called "The Flight of the Bumblebee." In it, Dr. Massie compares the seemingly insurmountable obstacles that Blacks faced trying to

achieve their goals to the lowly little bumblebee.

He notes that the bumblebee, by all accounts, is aerodynamically unsound and should not be able to fly. Yet, the little guy gets his wings going like a house afire. Off he goes to collect pollen from every plant his chubby little body can land on.

Bumblebees are the most persistent creatures. They don't know that they can't fly. So, they just keep buzzing around collecting pollen and making honey.

Like the bumblebee, you should never give up. Don't know that you can't fly and you will soar like an eagle. Don't end up regretting that you did not do something because you lost heart in the face of obstacles, or worse, because you were afraid to take the risk.

Risk-taking, in any form, is betting, whether you are playing bingo, trading stocks, buying a car, passing another car on the highway, starting a new career. All of these activities require you to take a risk.

You bet either on yourself or on chance. Many of us would rather risk against the odds and keep ourselves out of the equation. Of course, my position is you should keep yourself in the equation. It all boils down to "How far are you willing to leave the secure seat on the ground to get that apple in the tree?" Since I know each of you wants to aim for that top apple in the tree, let me give you some rules that you should follow.

Rule 1: Consider the odds and your intuition
Take yourself into account, influence the risk and outcome. Remember there is a difference between taking a chance when you

have no control over the odds and risking in a situation where you are a factor with some weight.

Work each situation on its own merits. Don't let a past history of risking stop your intuitive decisions or prevent you from seeing that the odds are in your favor.

Rule 2: Don't have an excessive fear of failure, disapproval from others, and fear of uncertainty

Consider the following words of Walter D. Wintle:

> If you think you are beaten, you are;
> If you think you dare not, you don't;
> If you'd like to win, but you think you can't,
> It's almost certain you won't.
>
> If you think you'll lose, you've lost;
> For out in this world you'll find
> Success begins with a fellow's will
> It's all in the state of mind.
>
> If you think you are outclassed, you are;
> You've got to think high to rise.
> You've got to be sure of yourself before
> You can ever win the prize.
>
> Life's battles don't always go
> To the stronger or faster man;
> But soon or late the man who wins
> Is the one who thinks he can!

Live everyday, my friends, to know yourself so that you can say,

"I am happy to be me. I like living with me."

I promise you, that no matter what you do in your life, you will find no greater treasure than faith, hope and confidence in yourself. In everything you do, do it to the fullest, and like the army, "Be all that you can be."

Continue to set high goals for yourself and pursue them with cheer and vigor. If you stumble, pick yourself up and remember what made you stumble. Look on these mistakes as learning experiences. And remember.

The only mistakes that are unforgivable are those we repeat.

The only challenges that are frightening are those we do not meet.

In the enduring words of Calvin Coolidge, "No person was ever honored for what he received. Honor has been the Reward for what he gave."

Challenges are opportunities in disguise. For every challenge, you have the opportunity to rise higher and higher.

Every challenge you meet and conquer will spur your confidence and self-respect.

Every obstacle you overcome will provide you with another stepping stone to reach for the stars.

To be a friend to others, you must first be your own best friend.

You should not lie, but if you do, never lie to yourself.

Don't compare yourself to others and shrink at what you see. You are unique. And what you do with that uniqueness will determine how and where you will carry yourself in the days ahead.

So stand with confidence and humility of spirit. Keep reaching forward, taking each step with all the energy you can muster.

Each one of you will develop and progress through your life at your unique pace.

Each of you will dream different dreams and each will win and lose your own special race.

Whatever endeavors you pursue, you must keep your intellectual curiosity alive. Learn all that you can about yourself, your fellow beings, and your universe. For, in learning, you are experiencing creativity. It will nurture your mind and soul. And you will bring great credit to youself, if, in learning, you seek truth and wisdom.

Be generous in all things, but mostly in sharing your joy. Challenge this sometimes unpleasant and mean-spirited world with a roaring sense of elation. Be clean in mind and spirit.

Know yourself and do those things that you do well, always keeping your own counsel and feeding your moral strength.

Don't ever sell yourself into the slavery of greed or power seeking. Keep your mind high, your ideals strong and unwavering.

Deceit, however small, will mar that great friendship you have with yourself, because you cannot hide from yourself.

You must face yourself every single second you are on this planet.

And if there is distrust within you, it will lay you low. So make up your mind, and try to dedicate yourself to being your best friend throughout your life.

If you are strong within, if you know yourself, you will always recognize the right to confront problems. There are no obstacles in life that cannot be overcome if you keep your wits about you and have a strong inner self.

There is a little poem by Edgar Albert Guest that Dr. Massie quotes (with a twist at the end) when he speaks to young Black people.

> I have to live with myself, and so,
> I want to be fit for myself to know.
> I want to be able, as the days go by,
> Always to look myself straight in the eye.
> I don't want to stand with the setting sun.
> And hate myself for the things I have **NOT** done.

Notes & Reflections

> " EVERYBODY CAN BE GREAT...BECAUSE ANYBODY CAN SERVE. YOU DON'T HAVE TO HAVE A COLLEGE DEGREE TO SERVE. YOU DON'T HAVE TO MAKE YOUR SUBJECT AND VERB AGREE TO SERVE. YOU ONLY NEED A HEART FULL OF GRACE. A SOUL GENERATED BY LOVE. "
>
> **- DR. MARTIN LUTHER KING, JR.**

40

Hon. Mary K. Bush

Giving It My All

CHAPTER FORTY

Hon. Mary K. Bush

Banker, Financier, Former U.S. Government Appointee to the IMF

Mary K. Bush has been President of Bush International since she founded the company in 1991 and has over thirty years experience in business, global financial institutions and government. The company advises on financing and business development strategies internationally. Ms. Bush is well known in international financial circles for innovative financial and business strategies that have helped transform markets. She has served three US Presidents — as the US Government's representative on the International Monetary Fund (IMF) Board, head of the Federal Home Loan Bank System and board member of Sally Mae.

Growing Up in Birmingham, Alabama

It was a very interesting environment to grow up in. Interesting because this was during the 1950s and 60s. Birmingham had the reputation of being the

> "I LOVED LEARNING. THAT LOVE STARTED WITH MY PARENTS."

most segregated city in America, and that's because the Jim Crow laws were very present and strongly enforced. It was also the time of the civil rights movement when Martin Luther King was coming to Birmingham to lead nonviolent protests and negotiate with the city fathers. Although King-led marches were nonviolent, the reaction was violence against Blacks with bombings of homes and churches. Most people know the story of the four little girls killed in a church bombing. That incident touched America's soul and sparked more intervention by the federal government. Two of those girls were friends of mine. This was one of the tragedies in our struggle for access to the opportunities that America offered to most of its citizens. The other side of the story was that my community did what I call message override. It started with my parents in my own home, but included my teachers, principals, neighbors and ministers — pretty much anyone who touched my life.

"Message Override"
The adults in our community gave us, the Black children, the message that "You can do and be anything you want in life, but you have to be twice as good." Their message was all about getting a top-notch education. Education was like a mantra. The message also was that we had to have the self-confidence, the knowingness, the wherewithal, the strength to do anything in the world. We understood that we had to push aside the very negative messages that were coming at us and absorb or believe what our community was telling us. That's what I did. Many of my friends did so too.

In Love with Learning — Parents as Role Models

I loved learning. That love started with my parents. My father had gone to school until he was, I believe, thirteen years old. He lived in a small farm town and had to stop school to work on the family farm when his father died. He was the only boy in the family, so the duty of farming fell on his shoulders. That hurt him all his life because he had such a curious mind, a love for learning and education. Although his formal education was cut short, he was one of the best educated people I've ever known because he read constantly. He read everything he could get his hands on and everyone in our orbit, when I was a child, marveled at the extent of his knowledge, especially about world events and history. His interest in international affairs and global events rubbed off on me.

My mother had grown up in the same small farm town. There were two high schools, one was for Whites, which went through the 12th grade, and one for Blacks, which went only to the 10th grade. So, she went as far with her formal education in her town as was allowed for Black kids. But she also kept learning on her own. I had great, great role models. Great examples of the power of knowledge. Somehow, my parents' love for learning was transmitted to me.

Through Reading: Capturing Visions of a New Reality

Reading helped me see a new reality — a wonder of opportunities that were not obvious to a Black kid in Alabama at that time. When I think back about reading *Advice and Consent* by Alan Drury, I had no interest in politics. But when I read that book, something struck a chord in me, and I said, I'm going to be there someday. This was in the powerful policy arena that affected international affairs. Just reading that book showed me the possibility of exerting influence on the world around me.

> "WHEN IT COMES TO ACHIEVING ONE'S GOALS, ATTITUDE IS 99% OF THE GAME. IN MY VIEW, THE WAY YOU THINK ABOUT THINGS AND WHAT YOU BELIEVE ARE FUNDAMENTAL TO DETERMINING OUTCOME."

On to Fisk University

Fisk University was wonderful for me. I was offered scholarships to several schools, one in Alabama. My father wanted me to be close to home and go to Tuskegee Institute in Tuskegee, Alabama. My mother and I prevailed, so, I went to Fisk. I received a small scholarship from Fisk. My father was a steelworker. Steelworkers made good money, so, we had a nice middle-class living. But a couple of other schools had given much larger scholarships that covered a large portion of tuition and room and board. When my father relented, despite the distance from Birmingham and the smaller scholarship, I was elated. After all, Fisk was one of the academic Ivy League of Black universities. But he allowed me to go even though it was a small scholarship. After a couple of semesters, the school had given me so much scholarship money that my father never had to pay another dime. So, he ended up sending me lots of spending money which I used mostly to eat at restaurants off campus, where the food was great. That made me happy.

Fisk was great for me. It was ranked as one of the top historically black colleges and universities academically. Achieving *magna cum laude*, Phi Beta Kappa, meant a lot for my opportunities in life. A major in biology and thoughts of medicine as a profession gave way when I took organic chemistry. But I fell in love with economics and my business courses. The business courses in my economics program captured my imagination so I decided on an MBA instead of PhD in economics or law school.

Grad School: The University of Chicago

University of Chicago Business School (now Chicago

Booth) was (and is) one of the top in the country. The school had joined with several major companies to offer fellowships to help enable Blacks to attend. There were about a dozen of us and we were welcomed into the hallowed halls. It was, and still is, a tough school — highly quantitative. Even a business psychology course had lots of calculus in the course. I had had very little math, and no calculus in my undergraduate economics program.

Conquering Calculus

The coursework was based on the assumption that we knew calculus. I went to the Dean of Students, and I said, I'm in trouble because they're putting all these math equations on the board, and I have no idea what they're talking about. His response — "Oh Mary, don't worry about it. We'll get you a tutor." The tutor they got me was a classmate. He had a master's in mathematics and chemistry. He was also Black but insisted that if he tutored me, the business school must also make his services available to anyone, black or white, who wanted his help. He ended up tutoring many of our black and white classmates. "You have a great aptitude for math," he said to me after a couple of sessions. "You just haven't had it before." He is my friend to this day. In fact, I am godmother to his three children. It led to a wonderful life-long, enriching relationship.

The Corporate Environment

Like most things in life, there were good parts and troubling parts of my early career years in New York. My time at Bankers Trust was the best. I was recruited by the bank after having gotten about 6 years' experience at Chase Manhattan and Citibank. Bankers Trust senior management had decided to transform their business model from an old-line "white shoe" firm (traditional & conservative) that was only in the second or third tier with Fortune 500 companies to a more aggressive, innovative style aimed at being a first-tier bank with big companies. To achieve that, they needed younger, hungry bankers. I was one of several that they recruited.

Placed in the New York City Division, with major NY headquartered companies as my clients or prospects, I reported to the Senior Vice President (SVP), Department Head. He was a deal man par excellence. In fact, he also had the Airlines/Aerospace Department reporting to him.

This was the mid-70s. John was in his 60s, gruff on the outside and many of the younger bankers thought he would not take well to a young, Black female on his team. Quite the contrary! I learned a ton from John about his negotiating good deals for the bank, about the importance of customer relationships and was mentored and supported by him in ways I will never forget.

Once an Executive Vice President from another major bank was coming to Bankers Trust to talk about a problem loan with one of the companies that I had been assigned. I said to John, "You must come to this meeting because Manufacturers Hanover is sending an Executive Vice President." I was the most junior officer – an Account Officer. John simply said, "Handle it, Bush. If you need me, I'll be here in my office." It turned out that I didn't need him. John did so many similar things to encourage my confidence and willingness to deal with the most senior people in our bank and in the companies that were my customers.

At another major bank, my first couple of years were great. My bosses were supportive. If there was an area where I was not performing well, like writing business letters, for instance, they were helpful and instructive. When the bank reorganized, I wound up reporting to someone else who was highly critical of almost everything. Even though I brought significant new business into the bank, small administrative things were a major deal in his mind and the criticism was harsh and frequent. There was also no attempt to provide constructive guidance.

So much depends on people — and whether they want to be constructive or not.

Experience in Government

Like most things I've done professionally, it was breaking ground in terms of being a Black or a woman in the position. In my first job in government, I was a political appointee working for the Deputy Secretary, second only to the Secretary of the Treasury Department. It was quite wonderful for me, working at such a high level at the treasury. I found myself working on policy issues that affected the banking industry, that would've affected things that I was doing when I had been a banker. I found myself sitting in a room with Paul Volcker and Don Regan, the secretary of the treasury and the controller of the currency. And this experience was excellent because even though I was quite junior, I was the one there with banking experience. They listened to my voice, my views, just as they did others.

Two years later, these same gentlemen, along with the White House Personnel engineered my appointment to the board of the International Monetary Fund. This was a Presidential Appointment subject to Senate confirmation. This experience took me solidly into the international economic arena as a US Representative on the Board that controlled over 19% of the voting power. I was able to exert influence through policies and IMF lending that promoted free markets in many places globally. Funnily, two people, one American and one Chinese, asked "Are you Black?" No Black American had ever been in such a position, so they evidently thought I was a person of color from some other country. My IMF experience was broadening and enriching. It was gratifying daily. I worked with people from almost every country in the free world.

Speaking of Attitude

When it comes to achieving one's goals, attitude is 99% of the game. In my view, the way you think about things and what you believe are fundamental to determining outcome. If you believe that you can do whatever you want to do in the world, then you are going to find a way to make it happen. That's what I had to do. Even though I'm saying all these experiences were wonderful, sometimes, I did have to ignore the attitudes, doubts, the naysaying of others and just keep moving forward. I had to focus on the messages from my parents and my whole community that I could do and be anything I wanted, that I had to work hard and perform with excellence.

Serving on Corporate Boards

Many of my board appointments have come from relationships already established. When a board was looking for a new Director, someone with whom I had worked or whom I knew socially, suggested me. A couple have come through executive search firms. At one, the company had already identified me as somebody they were interested in as a board member. In fact, their corporate secretary had seen my picture and my bio in the annual report or proxy statement of another board. And they saw my financial background and they said, "What about her?" And so, they had them check me out, but some have come through people that I've met or people with whom I've worked. One came through somebody I worked with at the treasury department. He was on a board. They were looking for a new board member with my skills and experience. He knew that my experience fit the bill, and so, the CEO got in touch. When serving on a board, the expectation is that you're going to contribute by calling on your experiences and your expertise to raise questions, to give advice to the executive team and the CEO. The value that I bring is my financial and capital markets knowledge and banking experience. As well, it's my government and public policy experience and my international experience, working in several markets around the world.

Definition of Success

What success means to me is living up to my own standards of excellence. At any time where I have felt that I was underutilized, that I was not using all that I have to offer, I didn't feel successful, but when I'm using what I have to offer and making contributions, then that is success. Success also means being a leader, knowing my strengths, and using them and having the confidence to build teams around me, that of people that complement my strengths.

Success is happiness. Being happy in doing what I'm doing, and I love what I do. At most of my jobs, I have loved what I do. And when I'm happy with it, when I love it, I know I'm really giving it my all.

A Piece of Advice – For the Person Lacking in Motivation

I would tell them to find something that they love. I'd say, find the part of the job that you love to do and be outstanding at that and figure out how to get the rest of the job done with as much excellence as you can muster. Or, if there is no part of it that you love, then you've got to go figure out what you really like and love doing and where you feel confident that you can make a contribution.

Notes & Reflections

> "NOT EVERYTHING THAT IS FACED CAN BE CHANGED, BUT NOTHING CAN BE CHANGED UNTIL IT IS FACED."
>
> **- JAMES BALDWIN**

INDEX

A

A Towel Sling, 248
AME Zion Church Sunday School, 223, 260
Abloh, Virgil, 293
Accenture, 126, 127
Accomplishment(s), 70, 89, 185, 229, 162
Accountability, 29, 270
Accountants, 29
Accra, 171
Accra New Town, 171
Addae, Amelia, 34
Adkins, Ellen, 81, 82, 84, 85
Advice and Consent, 316
African Diaspora, 16
Afro-American, the, 226
Alan Drury, 316
Alcohol, Sweet Rosey O'Grady, 239
Ali, Muhammad, 46
Allah, 145
Amagyei, Douglas, 176
Amanda Gorman, 96
Amelia Addae, 34
American Heart Association, 157, 200, 201
American dream, 43
Amherst, 125, 126
Amherst College, 125, 130
Amy Cooper, 58
Ancient Egyptians, 262
Anderson Consulting, 126
Angela Rye, 50
Angela Y. Davis, Dr., 186, 292, 293
Angelou, Maya, Dr. 19, 67
Anu, 107
Appiah, Kwame Anthony, Dr., 295
Apportionment, 235, 236
Architecture, 103, 104, 281
Arizona Board of Regents, 63
Arizona State University, 62
Armstrong High School, 82, 83
Art Museums, 214
Arun Gandhi, 111
Authenticity, 16, 57, 205, 276

Autonomy, 49
Autopsy, 239, 240
Axioms, 140, 141

B

Babbitt, Governor Bruce, 63
Bachelor's degree, 95, 136, 195
Bailey, John Watson, 224
Bankers Trust, 318, 319
Baptist, 42
Barack Obama, 103, 106
Barbara Jordan, 279
Beanie Sigel, 106
Ben Franklin, 231
Bias, 52, 262
Bill Gates, 300
Biomedical engineering, 170, 172, 175
Birmingham, 314, 315
Black Family, 18, 212
Black History, 6, 212, 232, 240, 261, 262
Bob Johnson, 300
Bobby Booker, 106
Booker T. Washington, 91
Booker, Bobby, 106
Boston, 123, 124, 174
Boy Scout(s), 226, 227
Brace, Heel Cord Stretching, 247
Brooklyn Dodgers, 232
Brown, Dr. Lucille, 83
Bryan Stevenson, 75
Bryant, Kobe, 161, 163
Bumblebee, The Flight of, 306

C

CMS Energy, 123, 130, 132, 133
Calculus, 318
Cambridge, 205
Cancer research, 180
Carbohydrates, 116
Career development, 189, 190
Caribbean, 16, 18, 24, 29, 32
Caribbean folklore, 16
Carpentry, 218

Carter, Jimmy, 112
Cartoons, 215, 225
Catalina, 214
Channeling, 270
Character, 20, 25, 26, 27, 100, 115, 154, 157, 226, 228, 276, 301
Chase Manhattan, 318
Chemistry, 5, 29, 89, 234, 287, 288, 317, 318
Choleric, 179
Christian, 28, 153, 176, 215
Christian Science, 215
Chuckles, 16
Church, Lighthouse International, 176
City College of New York, 172, 173
City Council of Philadelphia, 105
Civil War, 248
Clark, 64, 242, 244, 287
Clark, Douglas, 287
Clubfoot, 247, 253
Colin Powell, 204, 209, 300
Columbia Business School, 129, 131
Commitment, 158, 159, 167, 196, 202, 270, 277, 299, 304
Competence, 20, 25, 26, 27, 122, 127, 129, 132, 306
Confidence, 16, 26, 27, 131, 189, 200, 209, 291, 309, 310, 319, 322
Consumers Energy, 123, 132
Cooper, Amy, 58
Cooper, Christian, 58
Cornell, 125
Corporate Boards, 130, 202, 321
Cosmic Organism, 213, 219, 228, 229
Covid, 167, 175
Critical Thinking, 236, 261, 292
Crow, Jim, 74, 315
Cultivation, 290, 292, 294, 301

D

Dansoman, 171
Davis, Angela Y., Dr., 186, 292,

293
Dedication, 36, 116, 145, 235
Degree, Doctorate, 95, 100, 305
Denzel Washington, 289
Design(s), 6, 103, 106, 136, 137, 153, 163, 174, 294, 304
Dharma, 144
Diaspora, African, 16
Diversity, 5, 52, 53, 55, 56, 57, 58, 93, 246, 269, 270, 287
Diversity, Practical, 55, 58
Divination, Ifa, 17
Divine Consciousness, 265
Divine Logos, 225
Divorced, 170, 214
Doctorate degree, 95, 100, 305
Doctors, 4, 29, 124
Dogs, German Shepherd, 238
Don Newcombe, 232
Don Regan, 320
Doubt(s), 78, 296, 297, 299, 321
Douglas Amagyei, 176
Dr. Lucille Brown, 83
Dr. Martin Luther King, Jr., 48, 117, 145, 255, 275, 300, 312, 315
Dreams, 208, 286, 287, 288, 310
Dwarf Syndromes, 250, 253
Dwarfs, 249, 250

E

Ebong, Eno, Dr., 173
El Monte Medical Center, 240, 256
Elizabeth Town Crippled Children's rotation, 246, 247
Emergency, 153, 216, 244, 253, 257
Emotions, 82, 229, 241, 245
Empathy, 49, 178, 283
Employment Law in Business, 58
Empowerment, 270
Endurance, 66
Engineers, 29
Eno Ebong, Dr., 173
Entrepreneurship, 177, 178
Ethic, work, 62, 122, 127, 129,

INDEX

131, 132, 178, 188, 260
Ethics, Nicomachean, 41
Eve, 106
Excellence, 34, 41, 42, 53, 82, 85, 261, 277, 304, 319, 321, 322
Exclusivity, 184

F

Faith, 37, 77, 142, 149, 176, 277, 309
Faith Jenkins, 142
Family, Jewish, 215
Filipinos, 243, 244
Finance, 127, 128, 131, 133
Finland, 196
Fish, 116, 214, 225, 244
Fisk University, 317
Flight of the Bumblebee, The, 306
Florence, 220
Floyd E. Kellam High School, 82
Folklore, Caribbean, 16
Fortive, 130, 131, 132
Fortune 500, 318
Foundation, Freddie Mac, 48
Foundation, PETNA, 6, 33
Freddie Mac Foundation, 48

G

Gandhi, Arun, 111
Gandhi, Mahatma, 110, 111
Gang, 43, 112, 218
General Building Contractors Association, 106
General Colin Powell, 204, 209, 300
General Surgeon, 255
Genius, 214, 291, 292
Gentleness, 214, 223
George Floyd, 58
George Washington Carver, 231
German Shepherd dogs, 238
Germany, 282
Ghana, 29, 140, 149, 171
Global Medical Response, 202
GlobalWatch Technologies, 40

God, 28, 44, 77, 78, 94, 95, 98, 107, 111, 141, 145, 149, 179, 223, 228, 229, 259, 260, 264
Good Manners, 227, 228, 229
Gorman, Amanda, 96
Gospel, 43
Governor Bruce Babbitt, 63
Grace Dungee, 232
Graduate school, 22, 23, 30
Grandmother, 62, 107, 171, 173 195, 220, 221, 224
Grenada, 32, 33
Griot Mamadou, 15
GroupM North America, 188
Growth, Professional, 37, 100, 149, 150
Gynecology, 243

H

Haiti, 107
Handbook for Orthopaedics, 240
Harmony, 228, 229, 263, 265
Harris, Vice President Kamala, 113
Harvard, 58, 120, 126, 127, 128, 196, 197, 274
Harvard Business School, 126
Harvard Kennedy School, 196, 197
Harvard University, 120, 274
Harvey, Steve, 134
Healthcare, 174, 195, 197, 201, 282
Heart(s), 4, 35, 37, 57, 81, 111, 157, 200, 201, 300, 307, 312
Heel Cord Stretching Brace, 247
Helicopter dad, 179, 180
Henry VIII, 233
Higher Power, 45, 120
Hip-Hop Culture, 105
History, 4, 8, 16, 37, 48, 64, 89, 120, 145, 153, 212, 213, 232, 240, 249, 261, 262, 303, 308, 316
Hollers, 16
Homer G. Phillips Hospital, 239
Hope, 4, 149, 159, 263, 288, 309

Hostility, 245, 255
Howard Thurman, 108
Human resources, 69
Humility, 17, 163, 200, 310
Hurdles, 23, 24, 25, 184
Hypertension, 180
Hypoplastic odontoid, 250

I

Ifa divination, 17
Immortality, 228
Innovations, Therapeutic, 170, 174
Integrity, 18, 122, 127, 129, 131, 132, 154, 167, 204, 220, 228, 231, 259, 270, 277
International Monetary Fund, 314, 320
Internships, 204
Italian Opera, 215
Ivy League, 33, 125, 317

J

JAB Lifeskills Foundation, 211
Jackson, Ketanji Brown, 54
Jackson, Reverend Jesse Louis, 151
Jazz, 237, 240, 241, 248, 256
Jazz club(s), 241, 248
Jenkins, Judge Faith, 142
Jewish family, 215
Jim Crow, 74, 315
Jimmy Carter, 112
Joe Alexander, 255
John M. Tarbell, Dr., 173
John Watson Bailey, 224
Johnson Leadership Group, The, 81
Jordan, Barbara, 279
Jordan, Michael, 64, 155
Journal and Guide, 226
Journal of Bone and Joint Surgery, 250, 254
Judge Faith Jenkins, 142
Judge Lauren Lake, 86
Julian Bond, 146

K

Kaiser Hospital, 255
Kamala Harris, Vice President, 113
Kanye West, 199, 206
Kareem Abdul-Jabbar, 160
Kasoa, 171
Kellam High School, 82, 83
Kenneth Chenault, 129, 131
Keshia Knight Pulliam, 101
Ketanji Brown Jackson, 54
Kimpo, 242, 243
King, Dr. Martin Luther, Jr., 48, 117, 145, 255, 275, 300, 312, 315
Kobe Bryant, 11, 160, 162
Kobe Bryant mentality, The, 161, 163
Korean War, 231
Kwabenya, 171
Kwame Anthony Appiah, 295

L

Lake, Judge Lauren, 86
Langston Hughes, 288
Law of Sympathy, 263
Lawyers, 29, 124
Leadership, 6, 48, 52, 53, 61, 66, 81, 83, 98, 118, 119, 120, 153, 188, 197, 199, 200, 201, 202, 204, 209, 236, 281, 300, 301, 302, 303, 304, 305
Lee, Trymaine, 106
Legacy Destination, 212
Lifetime learning, 32
Lighthouse International Church, 176
Listening, 16, 17, 49, 207, 237
Litmus test, 27
Little Black Sambo, 232
Little Rock, 247
Longfellow, Henry Wadsworth, 189
Lorenzo Jones, 220
Los Angeles County Hospital, 240, 241
Lottery, U.S. Visa, 171, 172

INDEX

Louis Vuitton, 293
Love, 4, 42, 45, 111, 112, 202, 219, 220, 221, 222, 223, 231, 249, 251, 260, 276, 278, 282, 312, 315, 316, 317, 322
Loyalty, 25, 36, 167, 277
Lynn Swann, 82

M

M&A, 61, 129
MG, 244, 255
MIT, 205
MLK holiday, 64
Magnet high school, 194
Mahatma Gandhi, 110, 111
Make Excellence Routine, 261
Malcolm X, 191
Mama Clara, 220, 222, 223
Manager, Vada O'Hara, 60, 61, 64
Mandela, Nelson, 64, 66, 300
Mark Twain, 231
Marsalis, Wynton, 59
Martin Luther King, Dr., 48, 117, 145, 255, 275, 300, 312, 315
MassChallenge, 174
Massachusetts, 123, 170
Massie, Samuel, Dr., 306, 311
Master's degree, 166, 195
Material wealth, 141
Mathematics, 29, 89, 318
Maya Angelou, 19, 67
Mayor Sharon Pratt, 64
Ma'at, 228
McMaster University, 30, 33
Meat, 116
Mechanical Engineering, 171, 172
Media coach, 277
Medical Genetics, 249
Medical school, 30, 183, 211, 235, 237, 238, 243
Meharry Medical School, 211, 237, 238
Memoir(s), 18, 167
Mentees, 198, 212
Mentor(s), 41, 44, 74, 94, 95, 166, 185, 129, 202, 206, 302
Message Override, 315
Metaphysical, 70, 262
Metaphysical principles, 70

Michael Jordan, 64, 155
Microaggressions, 184
Mills, Rida Lamptey, 176
Minnesota, 213, 215, 218, 219, 221
Misjudgment, 66
Moans, 16
Model UN, 62
Model student, 84
Mofford, Rose, 64
Money, 22, 28, 31, 78, 105, 124, 149, 178, 214, 215, 216, 217, 220, 224, 226, 229, 236, 238, 240, 241, 244, 251, 252, 253, 259, 282, 317
Morehouse College, 211, 235
Morrison, Toni, 79
Mrs. Adkins, 81, 82, 84, 85
Muhammad (PBUH), 145
Muhammad Ali, 46
Multicultural society, 53
Murrell Dobbins High School, 103
Music festivals, 214

N

NU-ACCESS, 88
NYU, 202
National Institutes of Health, 173
National Minority Quality Forum, 198
National Public Radio, 95
National Science Foundation, 174
Natural, 130, 136, 200, 221, 222, 237
Naval Air Station, 83
Negativity, 74
Neil deGrasse Tyson, 267, 285
Nelson Mandela, 64, 66, 300
New Afrikan, 291
New Jersey Newark Beth Israel Hospital, 172
New Orleans, 6, 77
New Vista Magazine, 226
New York City, 115, 172, 239, 319
New York University, 193, 202
Newington Veterans Hospital, 253, 254

Nickel Producers Environmental Association, 148
Nicomachean Ethics, 41
Nike, 61, 64, 65
Noah, Trevor, 181, 272
Northwestern University, 88
Nurses, 29, 245, 246, 255
Nursing, 98, 167

O

Obama, Barack, 103, 106
Odu, 144
Opera, Italian, 215
Oppression, 52, 111, 145
Oprah Winfrey, 164
Optimism, 137, 156, 157, 303, 304
Orthopaedic Surgeon(s), 211, 240, 244, 245, 249, 250, 253, 255, 256, 257
Osu, 171

P

PETNA Foundation, 6, 33
Pancreatitis, 239
Pandemic, 167
Paradigm Shift, 45
Parker, Theodore, 145
Parks, Rosa, 121
Passionate, 112, 131, 184, 190, 196, 197, 202
Pathologist, 36, 240
Paul Rogers Family Foundation, 178
Paul Volcker, 320
Peace, 49, 53, 95, 228, 278
Pediatrics, 243
Pell grant, 65
Pennsylvania, 5, 42, 110, 144
Perfectionist, 179, 261
Perseverance, 57, 94, 95, 100, 119, 189
Persistence, 72, 73, 74, 167
Personal responsibility, 268, 270
PhD, 53, 90, 119, 174, 175, 195, 196, 200, 317
Philadelphia, 5, 103, 105, 106, 110, 112, 244
Philadelphia, City Council of, 105
Philanthropist, 21, 277
Phillips Andover Academy, 123, 130
Philly Green Man, 103
Philly Word Magazine, 103, 106
Philosophy of Life, 223, 260
Phlegmatics, 179
Physics, 29, 30, 270, 288
Piety, 120
Pittsburgh Steelers, 82
Planets, 218
Poor, 62, 78, 212, 236, 260
Potential, 29, 30, 74, 81, 84, 189, 269, 282, 284, 300, 302, 303, 304
Powell, Colin, 204
Powell, General Colin, 209, 300
Power, 10, 17, 36, 45, 65, 72, 73, 78, 120, 129, 130, 131, 184, 193, 198, 213, 229, 265, 279, 299, 305, 310, 316, 320
Practical Diversity, 55, 58
Practice, Orthopaedic Surgical, 253, 256
Pratt, Mayor Sharon, 64
Prayer, 97, 98, 124, 277
Pregnant, 170
Prejudice, 24, 184, 185
President Barack Obama, 106
President Bill Clinton, 95
Pride, 39, 40, 41, 42, 43, 45, 65, 184
Principles, 42, 44, 45, 57, 60, 61, 65, 66, 70, 120, 162, 163, 172, 188, 230, 236, 263, 265, 298
Principles, Metaphysical, 70
Private Orthopaedic Surgical Practice, 256
Privilege, 6, 52, 53, 66, 184, 185, 221, 296, 297, 299
Prize, Pulitzer, 106
Professional growth, 37, 100, 149, 150
Prototype, 205
Puberty, 43
Pulitzer Prize, 106
Purity, 45

INDEX

Q
Quietness, 223

R
Racism, 24, 52, 184, 201, 211, 221, 247, 256, 262
Radiologist, 249
Reagan, Ronald, 112
Reality, 17, 221, 230, 231, 235, 270, 282, 316
Research, cancer, 180
Respect, 17, 44, 81, 105, 205, 223, 224, 229, 256
Responsibility, 18, 28, 177, 198, 268, 269, 270, 302, 303
Reverend Jesse Louis Jackson, 151
Rida Lamptey Mills, 176
Riverside Seventh Day Adventist Hospital, 238
Ron Thomas, 256
Ronald Reagan, 112
Roosevelt, Theodore, 163
Rosa Parks, 121
Rose Mofford, 64
Rotation, Elizabeth Town Crippled Children's, 246
ROTC, 235
Roy Campanella, 232
Rye, Angela, 50

S
SAVOY Magazine, 65
STEM, 89
Sacrificing, 104
Sales, 69, 188
Sam Vick School, 224
Sambo, Little Black, 232
Samuel Massie, Dr., 306
Sanguines, 179
Scholarship(s), 5, 23, 317
Scientist(s), 30, 88, 89, 175, 193, 287
Self-confidence, 93, 167, 198, 292, 315
Self-esteem, 44
Self-respect, 40, 42, 44
Selfhood Greatness, 221, 222, 231, 235, 246, 258, 264
Selfless Service, 251
Sepsis, 180
Servant leadership, 118
Sharon Pratt, 64
Shortcuts, 152, 153, 154
Sigel, Beanie, 106
Sloan-Kettering Cancer Hospital, 239
South Africa, 64, 66, 95, 140
Spiritual Enlightenment, 228
Spiritual Entourage, 234, 253
Spiritual growth, 45, 100, 270
Sports, 25, 44, 61, 65, 82, 93, 126, 194, 253
Steve Harvey, 134
Steve Kopics, 250
Stevenson, Bryan, 75
Storyteller, 223, 277
Strategic planning, 69
Strengths, 27, 89, 94, 137, 180, 322
Stress, 53, 124, 125, 159, 263
Student, Model, 84
Suhum Secondary Technical School, 171
Surrender, 276
Sweet Rosey O'Grady alcohol, 239
Sword, 39, 40

T
Takoradi, 171, 172
Takoradi Polytechnic, 171, 172
Tarbell, John M., Dr., 173
Teachers, 29, 212, 216, 315
Teambuilding, 94
Temperament, 179
The Metropolitan Museum of Art, 88
The Salk Institute for Biological Studies, 162
Theodore Parker, 145
Theodore Roosevelt, 163
Therapeutic Innovations, 170, 174
Thomas, Ron, 256
Thurman, Howard, 108
Toni Morrison, 79
Toxicology, 148, 149
Traction-Suspensions, 246, 248, 252
Trymaine Lee, 106
Trevor Noah, 181, 272
Tropical Diseases, 243
Truth/truths, 139, 140, 141, 168, 221, 229, 231, 235, 301, 310
Tyson, Neil deGrasse, 267, 285

U
U.S. Visa Lottery, 171
UMOJA, 5, 110, 112
US Military Academy, 65
USA Air Force, 211, 241
Uncle Cecil, 213, 220
Unconditional Love, 220, 221, 222, 223, 231, 249, 251
United States Ambassador, 95
United States Marine Corps, 82
Universal Truths, 139, 140, 141
University of Arkansas, 212
University of California, Berkeley, 287
University of California, Davis, 73, 157
University of California, San Diego, 162
University of Chicago, 288, 317
University of Chicago Business School, 317
University of Cincinatti Health, 98
University of Connecticut, 253
University of Missouri, 74
University of Pennsylvania, 144
University of Waterloo, 33
Unselfishness, 45

V
Vada O'Hara Manager, 60, 61
Vegetables, 116, 226
Vice President Kamala Harris, 113
Vietnam, 243
Vince Roig, 62, 65
Violence, 111, 112, 315
Virgil Abloh, 293
Virginia Beach, 82, 83
Visa lottery, 171, 172
Votes, 78
Vulnerability, 276

W
Wallace H. Coulter Cardiovascular Lab for Cardiovascular Dynamics and Biomolecular Transport, 173
Washington, Booker T., 91
Washington, Denzel, 289
Weaknesses, 27, 94, 179
West Africa, 107
West, Kanye, 199, 206
Wharton, 144
Whipple, 239
White supremacy, 52, 293
Whoops, 16
Wiliams College, 125
Will Rogers, 231
William Penn statue, 111
Wisdom, 4, 100, 150, 176, 189, 207, 229, 235, 263, 264, 265, 276, 277, 299, 302, 306, 310
Worcester Polytechnic, 170, 175
Word Stories Surrounding African American Slavery, 213
Work ethic, 11, 62, 122, 127, 129, 131, 132, 178, 188, 260
World without Violence, 111
Wynton Marsalis, 59

X
Xandr, 188
X-rays, 249, 250

Y
Yale University, 254

Everett Ofori teaches Marketing, Management, Negotiation, and English for Specific Purposes (English Conversation, Medical English, Public Speaking, Business Writing, Medical Writing, etc.). Everett has conducted lessons or designed curricula for the following organizations.

- Accenture
- Actelion
- Ageo Central Medical College, Saitama, Japan
- Amazon Web Services (AWS)
- Asahi Kasei
- Asahi Soft Drink Research, Moriya
- AXA
- Bandai
- Barclays
- Becton Dickinson
- Boston Consulting
- Chugai
- Coca Cola
- Deutsche Bank
- Disney Japan
- ExxonMobil
- Fujitsu
- Goldman Sachs
- Gyao
- Hitachi Automotive
- Hitachi Design
- IIJ (Internet Initiative Japan)
- ING
- Johnson & Johnson (Janssen)
- JP Morgan
- JVC Kenwood
- Kistler
- Marubun
- McKinsey Japan
- Mitsubishi (Shoji)
- Mizuho Bank
- Moody's
- National Institute of Land and Infrastructure Management, Tsukuba, Japan (NILIM)
- Nomura
- Orix
- PriceWaterhouseCoopers (PWC)
- Quest
- Rakuten
- Recruit
- Reinsurance Group of America (RGA - Japan)
- Sekizenkai Nursing School, Shimosoga, Kanagawa
- Sumitomo
- Summit Agro International
- Suntory
- Tokyo International Business College, Asakusabashi, Tokyo
- Toyohashi University of Science and Technology
- Yokogawa Meters and Instruments
- Yokohama Child Welfare Vocational College (Hoiku Fukushi), Higashi Totsuka, Kanagawa

www.ingramcontent.com/pod-product-compliance
Lightning Source LLC
Chambersburg PA
CBHW081344080526
44588CB00016B/2374